PRAISE FOR MIKE SAGER

"Sager plays Virgil in the modern American Inferno . . . Compelling and stylish magazine journalism, rich in novelistic detail."
–*Kirkus Reviews*

"Like his journalistic precursors Tom Wolfe and Hunter S. Thompson, Sager writes frenetic, off-kilter pop-sociological profiles of Americans in all their vulgarity and vitality . . . He writes with flair, but only in the service of an omnivorous curiosity and defies expectations in pieces that lesser writers would play for satire or sensationalism . . . A Whitmanesque ode to teeming humanity's mystical unity."
–*The New York Times Book Review*

"I once described Mike Sager as "the Beat poet of American journalism." The title is still apt. For decades, he has explored the beautiful and horrifying underbelly of American society with poignantly explicit portrayals of porn stars, swingers, druggies, movie stars, rockers and rappers, as well as stunning stories about obscure people whose lives were resonant with deep meaning—a 92-year-old man, an extraordinarily beautiful woman, a 650-pound man. He became a journalistic ethnographer of American life and his generation's heir to the work of Gay Talese, Tom Wolfe, and Hunter S. Thompson. His imposing body of work today is collected in more than a dozen books and eBooks."
—Walt Harrington, author and past head of Journalism at the University of Illinois.

"Sager takes us inside different worlds in a way that is immediate, vivid, and dramatic. He doesn't hover 20,000 feet above his subject and just give you an overview—instead, you are right there on the ground level. He has a rare ability to get people to tell him things that they wouldn't tell other people, maybe not even themselves. He earns their trust by hanging around, by not pushing or manipulating. By being genuinely interested.

"Because Sager doesn't put any barriers between us and his characters, and because he renders them so thoughtfully and with such compassion, readers are allowed to focus on the drama of the stories. Above all, Sager doesn't get in the way of the story. He is not a commentator or a pundit. He doesn't analyze, his pieces don't have an obvious aim or thesis. His prose is so direct and unfussy, it's almost invisible, like a camera. And yet there is a propulsion to it because in almost every sentence you'll find a fact—that blessed newspaper training. The sentences flow with a definite rhythm, but Sager's style is unadorned with falsity, unburdened by over-interpretation. He's a natural storyteller. You never get the feeling he's there just to show off, only to entertain you."

—Alex Belth, editor of EsquireClassic.com and The Stacks Reader Series

ALSO BY MIKE SAGER

NONFICTION

Scary Monsters and Super Freaks:
Stories of Sex, Drugs, Rock 'n' Roll, and Murder

Revenge of the Donut Boys: True Stories of Lust, Fame, Survival, and Multiple Personality

The Someone You're Not:
True Stories of Sports, Celebrity, Politics & Pornography

Stoned Again:
The High Times and Strange Life of a Drugs Correspondent

Vetville: True Stories of the U.S. Marines at War and at Home

The Devil and John Holmes - 25th Anniversary Author's Edition:
And Other True Stories of Drugs, Porn and Murder

Janet's World:
The Inside Story of Washington Post Pulitzer Fabulist Janet Cooke

Travels with Bassem:
A Palestinian and a Jew Find Friendship in a War-Torn Land

The Lonely Hedonist:
True Stories of Sex, Drugs, Dinosaurs and Peter Dinklage

Tattoos & Tequila:
To Hell and Back with One of Rock's Most Notorious Frontmen

Shaman:
The Mysterious Life and Impeccable Death of Carlos Castaneda

Hunting Marlon Brando: A True Story

A Boy and His Dog in Hell: And Other True Stories

FICTION

Deviant Behavior, A Novel

High Tolerance, A Novel

Visit TheSagerGroup.net for more titles and authors

THE RISE AND FALL OF A SUPER FREAK

AND OTHER TRUE STORIES OF BLACK MEN WHO MADE HISTORY

BY MIKE SAGER

The Rise and Fall of a Super Freak: And Other True
Stories of Black Men Who Made History.
Copyright © 2021 Mike Sager

All rights reserved. No part of this publication may be reproduced,
stored in a retrieval system, or transmitted, in any form or by any
means, electronic, mechanical, photocopying, recording, or otherwise,
without the prior written permission of the publisher.
Published in the United States of America.

Cover design and cover art by WBYK.com.au
Interior design by Siori Kitajima, PatternBased.com

Cataloging-in-Publication data for this book
is available from the Library of Congress.

ISBN-13:
Paperback: 978-1-950154-40-1
eBook: 978-1-950154-41-8

Published by The Sager Group LLC
TheSagerGroup.net
In conjunction with NeoText
NeoTextCorp.com

THE RISE AND FALL OF A SUPER FREAK

AND OTHER TRUE STORIES OF BLACK MEN WHO MADE HISTORY

BY MIKE SAGER

Mike Sager met Rick James in 1995, while on assignment for Rolling Stone, within the thick stone walls of historic Folsom State Prison, where James was serving the final weeks of a sentence for assault, false imprisonment and furnishing drugs, the result of two separate crack-fueled incidents involving James, his then-girlfriend, and two other women. Upon James' release, the two men struck up a friendship on the outside. The expanded story of James' life, "The Rise and Fall of a Superfreak," was published in Sager's book, Scary Monsters and Superfreaks in 2003.

James died on August 6, 2004. In one of his last interviews, with the Atlanta Journal Constitution, James said he was reading Scary Monsters, "Because I'm in it, and because Mike wrote it, and Mike's a dear friend."

In an email to Sager, a mutual friend, LA set designer Averie S., wrote: "I was with Rick the night before he died and, believe it or not, he was singing your praises, showing your book to the other girl that was there. He went on and on about you for a very long time, talked about your experience in the crack house, etc., etc. The other girl and I were the last two to see him alive."

CONTENTS

The Rise and Fall of a Super Freak...1
    Rick James was one of the biggest names in the music industry—until he discovered freebase cocaine. An interview with the former King of Funk at Folsom Prison leads to a friendship with the author. His autographed copy of the original book containing this story, *Scary Monsters and Super Freaks*, was found beside his deathbed.

Requiem for a Gangsta...27
    Eric "Eazy E" Wright was a crack dealer who formed, along with icons Dr. Dre and Ice Cube, the seminal rap group Niggas Wit Attitude. Eazy's lifestyle set the bar for hip hop culture. But in the end, it wasn't guns or rivals that got him—shockingly, he succumbed to AIDS.

"Damn! They Gonna Lynch Us!"...47
    Black motorist Rodney Glenn King's videotaped beating, at the hands of the Los Angeles Police Department, would eventually touch off massive riots. A look at what happened that fateful night, from both inside and outside of King's vehicle.

The Real Rick Ross is Not a Rapper..73
    Freeway Rick Ross didn't invent crack. But he probably did more than anyone else to cause its spread. The way he sees it, Ross was a banker in a shadow economy—an American capitalist in the grand tradition of our country's rags-to-riches folklore, bringing jobs and riches to his people and himself.

THE RISE AND FALL OF A
SUPER FREAK

Rick James was one of the biggest names in the music industry—until he discovered freebase cocaine. An interview with the former King of Funk at Folsom Prison leads to a friendship with the author. His autographed copy of the original book containing this story, *Scary Monsters and Super Freaks,* was found beside his deathbed.

It must have been very late, around the time that night begins to turn on an imperceptible pivot and 2 o'clock becomes 6 in the morning. The place, if hazy memories serve, was the Red Parrot in New York City. The year was 1981. Or maybe it was '82. Definitely one of those, '81 or '82, toward the end of the Disco Era, a jangled, fuzzy, grandiose time when sex partners were changed more often than bed sheets and brain cells were slaughtered by the hundreds of millions. At clubs like Studio 54 and Xenon—the Studio for the Warhol Crowd, Xenon for the Eurotrash—beautiful people with pin-hole pupils were doing the Hustle and even the wild thing on strobe-lit dance floors, snorting crystalline cocaine out of little plastic bullets, gulping Quaaludes and champagne to dull the edge. What month? What year? Who the fuck can remember? The pace hadn't slowed since 1974. If you can remember exactly, you weren't there.

Rick James was there. His first rock and roll band had included Nick St. Nicholas, later of Steppenwolf. His second included Neil Young. He was a staff writer/producer for Motown when the Jackson parents brought their five sons through the door. Prince was once his opening act. James's trademark song, "Super Freak," sold more than 40 million copies in 1981. Later, a rapper named MC Hammer would cop the bass line of Super Freak for "U Can't Touch This." It sold millions more internationally.

By the time this night had come, Rick James was known around the world as the King of Funk, one of the biggest names in the music business. He had written and produced songs or albums for Stevie Wonder, Smokey Robinson, the Temptations, Teena Marie, Chaka Kahn, the Stone City Band, Eddie Murphy, and many more. His live shows were legendary. His long braids dusted with glitter, he strode the stage in thigh-high boots and spandex, crouching to accept joints and kisses from his adoring fans.

"Between Parliament and Prince, Rick James carried the banner of black pop over that fertile territory known as funk," wrote critic David Ritz. "As the seventies melted into the eighties, Rick was bad, superbad, the baddest of the bad. His orchestrations were brilliant, his shows spectacular. He worked in the celebrated R&B instrumental tradition—percussive guitar riffs, busy bass lines, syncopated horn punches—extending from Louis Jordan, Ray Charles, Ike Turner, James Brown, Sly Stone, and George Clinton . . . His funk was high and mighty, while his attitude stayed down and dirty. His eroticism was raw. He was an early gangsta of love, outrageous, unmanageable, both benefactor and victim of his own inexhaustible energy."

So, it must have been sometime in 1981, because James was at the height of his powers. He was in New York to celebrate the conclusion of a long national tour to support sales of *Street Songs*, the album that launched "Super Freak," as well as "Give It to Me Baby," "Ghetto Life," and "Fire and Desire." Sitting with him around the table at the Red Parrot—drinking Courvoisier and Perrier-Jouet, chatting up a seemingly endless stream of women—was James' usual coterie: seven or eight or nine of the boys in his Stone City Band, each one, like James himself, a black man standing over six feet tall, wearing long extension braids, leather pants, a rhinestone belt, a parachute-silk shirt, and python cowboy boots. They didn't call it a crew back then, but Rick James had one; he never went anywhere without the boys in his band. They were somewhere between a family and a musical commune.

For a while, they'd all lived together in the Hearst Mansion in Beverly Hills. Then James bought a ranch in Buffalo, and they all moved in together there. They rode James's Arabian horses (his favorite black stallion was named Punk), raced his ten snowmobiles, swam in the indoor pool, meditated amidst the jade sculpture and banzai trees in the "Oriental Room," played full court basketball or marathon games of Bid Whist, recorded in the basement studio, did drugs, lots of drugs, all the time. Rick James believed in drugs. As he'd said to the crew when he'd first assembled them: "Look at my lyrics to my songs. All of the songs are about drugs. They're about women and about drugs, and they're one and the same. That is the persona of this band."

When it started feeling a little crowded in the 28-room "ranch house," James bought the house next door, let everyone live there. He took care of his crew. If someone's momma had a medical bill, he'd give them the down payment. He never let a birthday pass without a catered party, though none bested the one he gave for the comedian Eddie Murphy, with hundreds of guests and a different kind of food in each of the themed rooms of the house.

James also let the crew drive his cars—he had more than a dozen, from Jeeps and Mercedes to an Excaliber and a vintage Rolls. Often, he'd give them upwards of $80,000 in cash to go shopping. He loved shopping. He'd stand in the middle of a store and point. Thirty pairs of cowboy boots. A half-dozen Cartier tank watches as gifts for different women. Ten exotic hides—including a lion, a bear, a zebra—for his "African Room." Intricately carved wooden furniture for his "Sausalito Room." Three hundred and sixty-five suits, one for every day of the year, even though he never wore suits, seemed to live in the same old pair of leather pants. He'd go to Bloomingdale's, in Manhattan, just to cause trouble. He'd walk through the store. A riot would ensue as women rushed for his autograph. One trip through Bloomies brought him face to face with Linda Blair, grown up considerably since her role in *The Exorcist*. Though he never talked about any of his women, other than to say how sweet or beautiful or thoughtful they were (he was known in private as a romantic), he did allude once to Linda's talents: "It's not just her head that swivels," he'd been heard to say.

Sometimes he'd get a buy and fly the whole crew to New Orleans for gumbo. He rented a yacht for a Caribbean cruise—fuel alone ran $30,000. Moonlit dinners for sixty on a terrace at a hotel in Hawaii. A $5,000 sushi dinner at Yamamotos in L.A. Along with the crew were the others, a cast of luminaries that included Dizzy Gillespie, Rod Stewart, Louis Farrakhan, Princess Elizabeth von Oxenberg, Steven Stills, David Crosby, Donny Osmond, Duane Allman, George Clinton, Sly Stone, Diana Ross, Willie Nelson, OJ and Nicole Brown Simpson, Denise Brown, Stevie Wonder, and Marvin Gaye.

And, wherever James went, there were women. They threw crotchless panties on the stage when he played. They climbed the gates and knocked on his door at three a.m. They arrived in cars sent for them. Teena Marie, Catherine Oxenberg, Catherine Bach, Grace Jones, Jan Gaye, hundreds of others: groupies, twins, mother and daughter teams, one time five women at once. All he had to do was open his bedroom door and point to someone at the party going on in his living room.

Now, at the Red Parrot in 1981, the security manager came over to James's table, told him there was someone upstairs who wanted to meet him.

"Who is it?" James asked.

"Can't tell you right here," said the manager.

"Well, whisper in my ear," said James.

"I think you'll want to meet him."

James shrugged his shoulders, Why not? He made a motion in the air with his finger like a trail driver: *Head 'em up, move 'em out.* The crew began to rise.

"Just you and one other person, if you please, Mr. James."

Rick James hovered there a moment, half out of his chair, slightly taken aback. Who, he wondered, could command more juice than the King of Funk himself? Now he was *really* curious. He gestured to his friend Taylor Alonzo, the manager of Xenon. They'd met one night at the club when the bouncers had refused to let James and his crew inside. Their friendship was solidified the day James took Alonzo along with him to buy a Rolls-Royce. James settled on a vintage silver blue Corniche. Then he asked the salesman to install wire wheels. "Rick," said Alonzo, "only a pimp would put wire wheels on that car." From that point on, James had come to rely on Alonzo to help him, as he put it, "separate the flash from the trash."

Now James and Alonzo followed the manager upstairs to the private room.

"Rick James, this is Mick Jagger."

Jagger rose unsteadily from his seat, at a table strewn with bottles of Cristal and Jack Daniel's. He was totally drunk. "Rick James!" slurred the legendary front man of the Rolling Stones. "Oh man! Super Freak! I just *had* to meet you!"

Fourteen years later, on a spring day in 1995, Rick James shuffles into a small office within the Gothic walls of Folsom State Prison, near Sacramento, Calif. He is chaperoned by a prison official, who will stay at his side for the duration of the interview. James's trademark extension braids are gone, his hair is cut short, combed forward to conceal a receding hair line. He's put on 30 pounds in jail—a combination of fatty prison food and care packages from his fiancée, Tanya Hijazi: tiny marshmallows, hot chocolate, jelly life savers (when she can't find Dots, his favorite), peanut butter and jelly, after dinner mints, raman noodles, and cartons of cigarettes to trade.

Now 48, James is serving the final days of a sentence for assault, false imprisonment, and furnishing drugs, the result of two separate crack-fueled incidents involving James, Hijazi, and two other women. To prison authorities, the King of Funk is just another resident of a two-man cell, with bunk beds and a shiny metal commode with no seat: James Ambrose Johnson Jr., Inmate #J29237.

James has passed his days inside the prison with grace, humor, and good behavior, prison officials say. He has worked in the prison library. He's nearly finished with his autobiography, *Memoirs of a Super Freak*, and he's written several screenplays, a lot of new music. From a computer in the library, he contributes to his personal web site, put up by some fans. He speaks every day by phone to Hijazi and their 4-year-old son, Tazman. Taz has long yellow ringlets, blue eyes, his daddy's sensual lips. He works occasionally as a model. He likes to bang on the piano and sing "Super Freak."

Rick James sits down and folds his hands demurely on the table. "I've been up, and I've been down," he says, a mixture of pride and pain discernible in his large brown eyes. "I been to hell and back. What you want to know?"

Monday afternoon, Aug. 30, 1993, California superior court, Los Angeles County. The defense lawyer, Mark Werksman, continues his cross examination on the witness, a woman named Mary Sauger: "Did (Tanya Hijazi) then commence to beat you again?"

"There was more hitting, yes," said the woman on the stand, one of two alleged victims of James and Hijazi.

"Was she doing it in such a way that suggested she thought it was a sexual act?" asked Werksman, turning toward the jury. His client, Rick James, was facing three life sentences: there were things these 12 workaday citizens had to be made to understand—they were a jury, yes, but they weren't exactly his peers.

"No," answered the witness. "It seemed they were getting their kicks out of hitting someone, beating someone up."

"There had never been any sexual involvement between you and Mr. James?"

"Absolutely not."

"Between you and Tanya Hijazi?"

"Absolutely not."

Werksman paused a moment, scanned his notes. The trial was entering its second week; the prosecution was still presenting its case, leaning hard on the lurid details. Werksman was doing his best to rebut.

Werksman was a Yale graduate, a former assistant DA, in his third year of private practice. Yet even in his rarified world, he had never before had a client come to the office with his girlfriend and his personal lawyer in tow. James had sat on the leather couch for a few minutes, then asked his lawyer for $5,000 in cash so he and Hijazi could go shopping. Here was a man at liberty on $750,000 bail, facing fifteen felony counts, including supplying cocaine, assault with a deadly weapon, false imprisonment by violence, torture, aggravated mayhem, and forced oral copulation. The district attorney had told Werksman: "I'm going to get him. He's evil, and I'm going to send him away for life."

James, however, appeared unfazed. In his constellation of reality, this whole case was a bunch of shit, period. "Fill each other in on what's happening," he'd said over his shoulder to his lawyers, strutting out of Werksman's office in thigh-high boots.

Since that first meeting, Werksman had begun to like James quite a bit. Reviewing the facts, getting to know his client, he began to sympathize with the King of Funk—and to disdain the alleged victims in the case. In his mind, the two women were drug users and groupies, drawn by the magnet of his client's fame from the ooze of the Sunset Strip, a five-dollar cab ride up Laurel Canyon Drive to James's mountaintop aerie, formerly owned by Mickey Rooney. The place was palatial, complete with guest house, gazebo, swimming pool, and prize rose bushes. James would tell Werksman that he had noticed the roses for the first time when police were carting him away in handcuffs. He'd spent the six months since he'd leased the house inside, mostly in his bedroom, sometimes in a walk-in closet, freebasing cocaine. For the past ten years, James had smoked up to $400,000 worth of the drug each year, most of which he cooked himself, though he had for a time employed an assistant he called Chef Boyardee.

Now, in court, Werksman cut his eyes to the witness, Mary Sauger, a brown-haired secretary at a small film company. She had told the jury that she'd visited James and Hijazi in a hotel room in Los Angeles to discuss working for his new label, Mamma Records. She said James and Hijazi beat her up. She also said she still had recurring headaches and constant throbbing in one eye. For her pain and suffering, she would later be awarded $2 million in civil suits filed against James and the hotel.

"Miss Sauger," Werksman began.

Suddenly, the quiet air in the courtroom was shattered by a series of thick, adenoidal snores.

All heads turned.

The King of Funk was sound asleep at the defense table, pencil still in hand, head lolling. His long extension braids, slicked into a pony-tail with Let's Jam jell, were leaving stains on the back of the state-issue leather chair. He wore a red uniform coat—a rocked-out

HMS Pinafore number with epaulets, stripes on the sleeves, and double rows of big gold buttons crowned with anchors.

The judge looked down at James, incredulous, the tips of his ears growing scarlet. A former LAPD police captain who'd attended law school at night, he'd served ten years as an assistant DA. This was the second time James had nodded out in his courtroom today.

"Mr. Werksman?" the judge intoned.

"Your Honor, may we have a sidebar conference please?"

***

James A. Johnson Jr. was born under the sign of Aquarius, the third eldest in a family of eight kids living in an all-black housing project in Buffalo, N.Y. His father was a handsome rogue with Native American blood who worked the assembly line at Chevrolet. "Mostly, he wasn't much of a dad," remembers James. "When I think of him, I think of the constant fights. He would beat my momma, and I'd sit at the top of the stairs with my brothers and sisters, crying, wishing I was grown up so I could kill him." He left the family when James was 7.

Momma was Mabel Gladden Johnson, known to her friends as Freddie. She had her first child at 13. Later she danced with Katherine Dunham's troupe, worked as a showgirl at the Cotton Club. She regaled James with stories of her days as the queen of the Rum Boogie during the Harlem Renaissance.

In time, Momma moved her family to a housing project across town, peopled mostly with Irish and Italians. James remembered cross burnings, rocks through windows. A gang of greasers claimed the turf near the corner store; they terrorized James and his siblings until the day his eldest brother Carmen came home from prison and whipped their butts. James remembers his father showing up to join the fight; it was the last time he ever saw him.

By day, Momma mopped floors. By night, she ran numbers for the Italian mob, James says. Though she made a lot of money, she kept the cleaning job and the apartment in the projects as a cover, she would later explain to her son. There were rats and roaches in their apartment, but the refrigerator was well stocked, the kids had nice clothes, Momma always had a nice car. Though James would come, over time, to regard his mom as his best friend in the world, he remembers his childhood being rough, Momma beating him with a knotted electrical cord "to let out her frustrations," he told a court therapist.

James attended Catholic school for a time, was an altar boy. In public junior high, he played football and basketball, took drum and trombone lessons, marched with a hi-stepping drill team, hung on the corner with friends singing do-wop and drinking Thunderbird. Entering his teens, James joined a gang, began smoking pot, committing petty crimes. Then his closest brother, Roy, was knocked from his new bike and dragged down the street by a car. Roy was in the hospital in a body cast for a year. Momma visited every day. In the family, Roy was known as the smart one. He would later become a lawyer. James was known as the troublemaker. James felt his mom somehow blamed him for Roy's accident. Between her jobs and visiting Roy, James hardly ever saw her. He began skipping school. Sometimes, he'd steal money from her purse and take a bus to New York City, haunt the coffee houses in Greenwich Village. At 13, police in Rochester found him hiding in the bathroom of a bus and he was placed in a juvenile home for several weeks. "Momma finally came to get me," James recalls. "She asked me why I was running and what did I hope to find. I told her with tears in my eyes, I didn't know. I just wanted something more out of life. She would just look bewildered and cry. I hated to see my mother cry."

At about 14, following a gang rumble in which a boy was shot, James was sentenced to several months in juvenile detention.

It was in high school that he settled on his life's course. "I signed up for a talent show. I was center stage, alone. A spotlight on me and I started off with a bongo beat. Then I began to sing out this chant. I asked the crowd to sing along and they did. As they sang, I picked up my mallets and my tom drum and played this funky beat, adding rim shots. . . . The crowd chanted louder and louder until the auditorium seemed to be moving. The rhythm seemed voodoo-like. I don't remember how long I played before I started dipping off the stage while the audience continued the chant. The feeling of the crowd singing, the people dancing in the aisles, calling out for more . . . All of it cast a magic spell on me. From that day on, music was my life."

James eventually dropped out of school. At 15, with his mother's permission, he joined the U.S. Naval Reserves. His obligation was two weekends a month. He went the first time to basic training with his stripe sewn upside down. At home, James started a group called the Duprees. They sang Motown tunes, practiced their harmonizing every day. He also had a jazz quintet; James played drums on covers of Herbie Hancock and John Coltrane, and on funky, straight-ahead bebop. The groups did well; they started to gain a local following. The big problem was that the gigs were on weekends. James failed to attend his mandatory reserve meetings.

In 1964, after numerous warnings, James was placed on active duty, ordered to report to the USS *Enterprise*. Though he made it to Rochester, where he was supposed to register, he overslept. Faced with disciplinary action, he fled to Toronto.

In the mid-sixties, Toronto was home to Yorkville, a gathering spot for draft resisters, a petri dish for a nascent coffee house, and rock scene similar to the one developing in New York's Greenwich Village. Many future big names were there: Richie Havens, David Clayton-Thomas, Joni Mitchell, Gordon Lightfoot, Kenny Rogers.

New in town, James was walking down the street in his Navy uniform when he was accosted by several men in sharkskin suits. A fight ensued; three hippie strangers came to James's rescue. Among the trio were Garth Hudson and Levon Helm, later of The Band. One of the guys took him to a coffeehouse; James ended up performing with the group on stage, singing "Stand by Me" and "Summertime." The leader of the group, Nick St. Nicholas, asked him to join.

As James had no civilian clothes, it was decided that the band would wear the contents of James's dirty bag—denim bellbottoms, blue workshirts and dixie cups, white sailor caps. They billed themselves as the Sailor Boys. Being AWOL, James took a new name, Ricky James Matthews, after the dead cousin of a friend. He became well known in Yorkville as Little Ricky. The Sailor Boys begot the Myna Birds, financed by a wealthy Englishman who fancied himself another Brian Epstein, the manager behind the Beatles. He dressed the group in yellow and black leather outfits, had them cut their bangs into a V. He staged publicity stunts, paying women to chase the Mynas through department stores. Soon, Neil Young joined the band. There were Canadian TV appearances, sold out concerts, groupies swooning in the front row.

Motown called: The Mynas were signed. They recorded a single written by James and Young. Then Motown discovered that James was AWOL. The record was not released; James was advised to turn himself in.

Nine months later, sitting in the Brooklyn naval brig, awaiting his court-martial, James picked up a teen magazine. There was an article on the "new California sound." Mentioned were Buffalo Springfield, featuring his old Myna partner Neil Young; and Steppenwolf, with Sailor Boy Nick St. Nicholas. "I was happy, sad, and pissed, all at the same time," James recalls. "I decided I'd been in the brig long enough." He busted out.

Eventually, at the urging of his momma—who said her phones were being tapped by the FBI—James turned himself in. He received a dishonorable discharge and several more months in the brig. Following his release, he went directly to California. He hooked up with his old friends, made new ones: David Crosby, Steven Stills, Jim Morrison, Donovan, Michelle Phillips. After a few months of dropping acid, smoking pot, jamming with other bands, collecting free love, James decided to fly back to Toronto and assemble a group of his own.

Within hours of arrival, James was in a club in Yorkville when the owner told him someone wanted to see him outside.

"Welcome back to Canada, Mr. Johnson," said one of the two Toronto cops who were waiting on the sidewalk. James was charged with possession of stolen property and jailed without bond, detained by the Canadian immigration department. Nine months later, he was deported.

Back stateside, Motown took James on staff, put him up in a hotel. His first project was with Tommy Chong, a guitarist who would later become a comedian and actor. The song was an interracial love story about Chong's wife and the birth of his daughter, Rae Dawn.

Eventually, James quit Motown, unsatisfied with the glut of talent in line ahead of him. For the next several years he kicked around the U.S. and Canada. He was a pimp for a while, he says. He smuggled cocaine from Colombia and hash from India, where he also took time to learn the sitar. In 1977, he finally got the financial backing to record an album at the Record Plant in New York City. After hawking it himself, enjoying local success, he was signed once again by Motown. The single "You and I" went to No. 1 on the R&B charts. It became the anthem at Studio 54. The album, *Come Get It*, was touted in trade magazines as the year's biggest album by a black artist.

About this time, James attended two performances that would shape his public style as the King of Funk; spandex jumpsuit, superhero boots, bare chest, big bulge, long extension braids. The hair concept came from a troupe of Masai Dancers. Their coiffures were elaborate configurations, braided with extensions of horse and lion hair. For $300, James had the troupe's stylist give him a new look: long, flowing braids with beads and bangs. Then, he saw a performance by Kiss. They wore tight black costumes, had big-time pyrotechnics going on, loud drums on risers 25 feet in the air. "I knew then that my concerts would be like the Fourth of July—a big party. I knew what my image would be," James says.

With *Come Get It* hitting double platinum, James received his first royalty check, $1.8 million. He leased a mansion formerly owned by William Randolph Hearst. He set up a rehearsal studio in the great room, began assembling a permanent band.

Danny Lamelle was the arranger and director of the horn section of what came to be known as the Stone City Band. Between 1979 and 1986, he made 16 albums with James, nine of which James produced for such finds as Teena Marie, the Mary Jane Girls, and Process and the Do-rags. Making his records, James was exacting, demanding, obsessive, instructive. He had an instinct, an ear. He'd order tracks recorded again and again until every note was perfect. He brought out the best in everyone. Once, Lamelle remembers, just after a marathon recording session, James and the band were headed from L.A. to Sausalito in a Winnebago. They were drinking and smoking herb, listening to the final cut of "Give It to Me Baby," which was being sent to NY the next day for mastering. "We're laying back, listening to the song, when suddenly Rick has the driver stop the Winnebago. 'Did you hear that?' he asked us. And we're like, 'What?' He rewound the tape again and again, playing this one section. We sat on the I-5 for an hour. He cursed us out, fired us, threatened to drop us off on the side of the highway." During the entire time, no one in the band had an inkling of what the problem was.

Finally, James condescended to explain: in one section of the song, for several bars, the horns, which were supposed to be stereo, played only out of one speaker. "Y'all would have mastered this, printed it, and it woulda been out there and it woulda been wrong," he told the band. "My shit gotta be perfect."

"We used to rehearse, boy," says Candi Ghant, one of the original Mary Jane Girls. "The band would rehearse from 12 to 5. Then the girls would rehearse from six till two in the morning. Whatever it took, you know, with him there were no hours. We had a choreographer we worked with five days a week. We had a vocal teacher. Rick was like a slave master. We didn't party, we didn't go wild. We weren't supposed to have boyfriends. After the shows it was interviews, pictures, and we was escorted to our rooms. And they would take a bed check to make sure you were in there. He was like a boss, a husband, a mother. He was hard on us. But if he did something to hurt your feelings, in the end he always gave you a gift to say he was sorry."

In 1980, the entire entourage moved onto a seven-acre ranch near Buffalo. When they weren't working, James and the crew played equally hard. The house was equipped with a jukebox, a stereo system in almost every room, a pool table, video games. James was competitive. He'd bet hundreds of dollars on Galaxian, his favorite video game. When other groups were touring the area, basketball tournaments were held. James played power forward, was a good assist man, never a ball hog. Grandmaster Flash fielded a team against James's crew, as did Cameo and Luther Vandross's band. Eddie Murphy was also a frequent player. James's teams always won.

Though James employed a 24-hour, on-call chef (for a time it was one of his sisters; most of his family was on the payroll, including his momma), he often woke early and cooked enormous breakfasts:

eggs, pancakes, bacon, grits, toast, milk. He was a consummate host. At parties, he'd go from room to room, checking to see if there was enough food, enough drink, enough toilet paper in all the bathrooms.

Frequently, James would go to New York City, driven in a van or in one of his cars at high speed by an off-duty New York State patrolman who was on his payroll. He'd pick up Taylor Alonzo, manager of Xenon, and check into the Plaza Hotel. Then the party would begin. "He charmed everyone he met," says Alonzo. "He was always on. He loved this Indian restaurant Bombay Palace. He'd do his Indian accent the whole time he was in there. Or he'd just start singing at the table. I remember once he sang Beatles' songs the whole evening."

"Rick was kind of a connoisseur," says his brother, Carmen Johnson Sims, who headed James's security staff for several years. "He liked his Japanese food, his French food. He used to amaze me. We'd be in Mr. Chow's in New York, and he could order in French. He was down with the wines too."

Back at the Plaza, James would usually have a whole floor at his disposal. Says Sims: "We had guys stationed at the elevators to give us privacy and control. We'd have suites for all the crew, and two or three suites that were loaded down with groupies—the choice ones, the weeded-out ones. We called them the 'Stockpile.'" The parties would go until dawn. Often, Alonzo remembers, James would be the last one left standing. Stepping over the sleeping bodies, James would come over and wake Alonzo. They'd leave the suite, walk for hours through Central Park.

James was a regular at Studio 54, the reigning Mecca of Disco. He partied with supermodels Iman and Janice Dickinson, with whom Alonzo says he had "this *Fatal Attraction* relationship. He'd sometimes have to duck her, if you know what I mean." Peter Max, Ted Kennedy Jr., Andy Warhol, Jim Brown, Ben Vereen, Robin Williams, Jack Nicholson—James partied with everyone. Drugs, of course, were abundant. In his own words, James "had never done a drug he didn't like." His second single, "Mary Jane," was a love song to marijuana. Cocaine, however, was his drug of choice. By now, he was snorting about an ounce a day.

"Nobody knew coke was so bad at the time," says James. "Nobody knew anything about detox. There was no Betty Ford. When you snorted it, you could function just fine. We made records doing it, sitting at the console with ounce-full bags. It was just a part of life. Everybody kept a big box full of pills: Quaaludes, Valium, Halcyon. Dishes of cocaine, trash bags of weed, bottles of bourbon. It was all about, hey, good drugs, leather clothes, horses, cars, and fucking women. That was the criteria for the times. When we went on tour, my accountants figured out that we were spending like $250,000 on coke for everybody. They wrote it off as payment to this employee they named Jose Coca."

In the spring of 1981, James and Lamelle went to see Sly Stone in San Francisco. Sly was freebasing—sitting in a back room at a recording studio with his butane torch and his pipe, totally out of it. "When we left, Rick turns to me and says: 'Look, we smoke herb, we snort, we drink. But we will never do this. Sly is a legend. He's in the history books. Now look at him, and he did this to himself with this drug. We can never allow this to happen to us.' And right there, on the spot, we made a bond that this would never be."

A few days later, in a hotel room in Chicago, James took his first hit of freebase, supplied by one of the leaders of the fabled Blackstone Rangers.

And a few days after that, James flew back out to the coast, went to see Sly again. This time, he joined him in the back room. They stayed in there for a solid week.

For the next ten years, with brief periods of sobriety, James would smoke up to $10,000 worth of coke a week. He had a special briefcase for his paraphernalia. It was the only thing he always carried himself.

Incredibly, he continued to make hit records. In the five years that followed "Super Freak," James recorded four albums, earned two Grammy nominations. He produced "Ebony Eyes" with Smokey Robinson and "Standing on the Top" with the Temptations. He made the rounds of the television shows—from *The Merv Griffin Show* to *The A Team*. He was a presenter at the Grammy awards; *People* magazine named him to its best dressed list. He was also black music's most outspoken voice in the fight with infant MTV over equal time for black artists, a powder-keg of an issue at the time.

In the inner circle, however, things had changed markedly. "It wasn't a group effort anymore. We would be downstairs working and Rick would be partying in his bedroom. He would come down, listen, give his okay, or tell us to change something. Then he would disappear again," says Lamelle. "He was the classic Dr. Jekyll/Mr. Hyde. When he was smoking, he became downright abusive. Like, before, he may have been blunt, but he was never brutal. Now the words were like knives. You started taking it personal."

In time, things around the ranch began to erode, says Linda Hunt, who still works as caretaker of the place. "He got rid of the horses because he didn't ride anymore. He stopped paying for rental cars for people. The games, the trips with the whole crew, everything stopped. Fewer people worked here; fewer people lived here. He just didn't want them around. I guess it was paranoia from the drugs."

"I found myself isolating more and more," James writes in his autobiography. "If I wasn't in my room (where my housekeeper would leave food by my locked bedroom door), I was flying here and there in private planes getting high in the clouds. I was slowly but steadily losing control. I'd stay up six or even ten days straight. I had my staff put aluminum foil on all my windows so no sunlight could get in.

"I OD'd a couple of times, but it had been kept a secret. My security or a doctor I had on the payroll would bring me back. My life on the inside was dark and lonely, while on the outside I always made it look like I was together. I felt like I was the loneliest person in the world. When I would try to explain my pain to friends, they would just laugh. 'You're Rick James,' they'd say. 'It will be all right.'

"It got to the point where I lost my desire to write music. When it was time for my eighth album, I had nothing in my head. It seemed my creativity was gone, lost in a world where smoke was all I could create, and rock coke was the only music I understood."

***

At 4 one July morning in 1991, a young woman came up the hill to James's house on Mulholland Terrace; one of hundreds of people who had made the trip in the four months he'd been living there. This one was a blonde with a southern accent. She called herself Courtney.

Courtney's real name was Frances Alley. Twenty-four years old, she'd recently dropped out of a drug rehab program near her home in a small town outside Atlanta. Now she was working at a massage parlor in Hollywood, living in a transient hotel on the Sunset Strip.

Alley was visiting a run-down motel on the Strip called the Seven Star when she encountered a friend of James's named Kathy Townsend. Townsend was a former backup singer who'd descended into a life of drugs. She was leaving the motel room occupied by a friend of hers, a pimp. She'd wanted to borrow some of his girls to take to James's house. James, she'd told the pimp, had been very unhappy because his mom was dying. Some girls would cheer him up, she'd said.

The girls would also serve to get Townsend some free drugs. She visited James occasionally, would smoke coke for free for days. Everybody at James's smoked for free. There was always a couple of dealers attending the 24-hour party going on in the living room. They often charged him as much as $100 above the going rate for an eight-ball. As a binge went on, they'd add more baking soda to the weight.

Townsend, unlike most of the hangers-on, would try to do something for James in exchange for the drugs. She'd help around the house cleaning or cooking, running errands. Or she'd bring him a girl. James wasn't interested in Townsend that way. He called her, lovingly, "Fat Ass."

At any rate, the pimp refused Townsend's request, fearing his girls would never return. Upset, Townsend slammed the door behind her, whereupon she encountered Alley, who was knocking at that moment on the door of a room occupied by a Mexican coke dealer. This was the first time Townsend had ever seen Alley: she looked kind of pretty in the dark. Townsend asked Alley if she wanted to go to Rick James's house and do some drugs. Oddly—or maybe not so oddly, this was the second time in her two months in L.A. that someone had offered to take Alley to James's house to party. "I guess I just felt like I was destined to meet him," she would later say.

For the past five years, James had been unable to work. At first, his problems were legal. In 1987, James filed a suit against Motown, seeking $2 million and a release from his contract. Motown, meanwhile, was suing James for not fulfilling his contract. As the lawyers exchanged paper, as the civil suits wended their way through the legal system toward a court date, James moved to L.A., on call for his lawyers. He spent his time at home, sucking on his glass pipe. He called it the devil's dick.

Then, just as the suits were being settled, mostly in James's favor, he learned that his mom was dying. Her passing, he says, "was a stunning, terrible, terrible experience for me. She was my best friend, the best woman I've ever met in the world."

James became depressed. He'd smoke straight through a week or ten days at a time, women coming and going through the binge. Then, he'd take a handful of Halcyon and sleep a few days. Then he'd wake up and start again. Month after month. "One of the things about it that really attracted me was the consummation of time with basing," James says. "The ritual of preparing it, the ritual of doing it, the manipulation and almost mind control that you would have over everything and everyone while you were doing it. It was complacent. It consumed your mind. There wasn't time to think about everything that was bothering me."

Arriving at James's house, Alley was admitted to James's bedroom right away. She partied with James and his girlfriend, Tanya Hijazi, for six straight days and nights. James liked Alley, he would later say, because he'd never before met a woman who could smoke as much coke as he. Finally, when Alley got tired, James had one of this staff make her up a bed in a spare room. She was given a boom box and a night table to make things homey.

After sleeping for 24 hours, Alley woke up, walked naked down the hall to James's room. She said hello, then went to the kitchen to get a soda and a candy bar. When she came back to James's room, she recounted, they smoked a little freebase. Then, according to Alley, James discovered that an eight-ball of cocaine—3.5 grams, about $200 worth—was missing. He accused her of stealing it, she said.

According to Alley, James became enraged. He ordered Hijazi to bind Alley to a chair with some neck ties, one from Dior, the other from Barneys. Then, Alley alleged, he smacked her across the face with a gun and poured rubbing alcohol on her waist, stomach and legs. An interrogation ensued for the next several hours, Alley alleged, during which James continued smoking cocaine. After a hit, she alleged, he'd place the hot pipe on her legs or stomach, causing small circular burns. At one point, she alleged, he ran a hot butcher knife along her leg, causing severe burns. During the interrogation, she told police, Hijazi stroked and held her hand; later, she told police, she was forced to have oral intercourse with Hijazi, after which Hijazi urinated on her, causing great irritation to her burns.

Finally, after several hours, Alley convinced James of her innocence.

"Okay, fine then," James said. He proffered his pipe. "You wanna hit?"

"Sure," said Alley.

The party resumed.

Two days later, after coming and going several times from James's house—where she was living as a guest, telling people she was James's new girlfriend—Alley went to the hospital for treatment of her burns. Doctors called the police.

James and Hijazi, who was then 21, were arrested and charged with nine felony counts, including supplying cocaine, assault with a deadly weapon, aggravated mayhem, torture, false imprisonment, and forcible oral copulation. Bail for James was set at $1 million; Hijazi's was $500,000. Both spent three weeks in jail. Their lawyers claimed that Alley had been burned and tortured by a pimp, that she and the police were targeting James with trumped-up allegations due to his status as a superstar.

By November 1992, James and Hijazi were out on reduced bail, living with her mom in the L.A. suburb of Agoura Hills, awaiting trial. A son, Tazman, had been born in May of that year. One weekend, Hijazi and James left the baby with her mom and went to the St. James Club and Hotel for a little break. The usual partying ensued; a young secretary with experience in the music business named Mary Sauger was invited over to discuss a job at a new label James was starting. It was to be called Momma Records.

Sauger arrived around 10:30. The trio smoked coke, drank, talked, ordered room service, made phone calls to friends on both coasts. Sometime in the early hours, Sauger would testify, Hijazi became angry and slapped her. James joined the fracas, grabbing Sauger by the throat, dragging her into the bathroom, beating her. When she passed out, she told police, Hijazi and James revived her with ice water.

The torture and beating continued, Sauger said, through a room change—other guests had complained of the noise. Hours after that, she was finally allowed to leave, taking a cab home with $5 Hijazi had given her. Two days later, Sauger went to the hospital. A doctor called the police. Hijazi and James were arrested again. Prosecutors combined the two cases and brought James to court.

***

"Will Mr. Johnson please rise?"

On January 7, 1994, James stood in his place behind the defense table, his lawyer at his side, waiting to learn his sentence. Hijazi sat behind him in the gallery with Tazman and her mom. She had already pleaded guilty to one count of assault with a deadly weapon. She was due to begin serving a two-year sentence. In her purse, she had a set of gold wedding bands. The judge had hinted that he'd possibly consent to marry the pair before they went off to jail.

Though he had faced 15 felony counts, James was found guilty of only three: false imprisonment, assault, and furnishing cocaine—all of those charges stemming from Mary Sauger's visit to the St. James Club. The jury found him not guilty on three other charges, deadlocked on all the rest. James faced a maximum of nearly nine years in prison.

However, while James was awaiting sentencing, information surfaced that an investigator from the district attorney's office may have been having a love affair with a woman in jail who'd been called as a witness against James. Further, it was alleged, he was supplying the woman with heroin during the trial. The woman, who was serving time on burglary charges, had testified about a night in which James supposedly smoked a kilo of cocaine and then broke her arm. James contended he'd never met her. Hijazi, however, knew her well. They'd shared a jail cell.

Now, with an investigation of the alleged police misconduct underway, the district attorney's office was forced to cut a deal. James would be sentenced to five years and four months. With good behavior, he'd end up serving about two years. Given the development, the judge had to reduce Hijazi's sentence as well, cutting it in half from the original four years. She would end up serving a little more than one year.

"Mr. Johnson," said the judge, looking down from his bench, addressing the King of Funk by his legal name, "when this is through, I want to rub your tummy, because you are the luckiest man on earth, and I want some of that luck to rub off on me. If I'd had my way, I'd have thrown away the key."

With that, the judge banged the final gavel on People of the State of California vs. James Ambrose Johnson Jr., a.k.a. Rick James. Then he turned to the other business at hand, James's and Hijazi's nuptials.

The judge asked the lovebirds to stand. He regarded them a moment, the tips of his ears growing red. "There is no way on God's green earth that I will marry you," he said. He smiled, satisfied. Then he banged the gavel. Next case.

***

Back at Folsom State Prison, the corrections officer chaperoning the interview looks at his watch and coughs. The rules specify that press visits may last no more than 90 minutes. Inmate #J29237 must follow the rules. He must eat, shower, sleep, work, exercise when they tell him, where they tell him. His mail is opened and read before he gets it. Some of the items in his care packages are always missing. Phone calls must be collect; time limit: fifteen minutes. His visitors are closely screened. Hijazi, a convicted felon now, is barred from visiting. James hasn't seen her or Tazman for three years, since that last day in court. A wedding is planned upon his release.

July 1996: That is when he hopes to walk out the gates a free man. Though he has declared personal bankruptcy, there is money enough left in the coffers of his record company to ensure a comfortable launching pad for Phase 2 of his career. Things look promising, he says. *Bustin Out: The Best of Rick James*—a collection released in 1994 by Motown, has done well. His collaboration with Evan Dando on a Lemonheads song was touted by critics as the "most powerful cut" on *Come On Feel the Lemonheads*. Another collection of previously recorded songs, entitled *Wonderful,* is due out from Reprise Records later this year.

Though the King of Funk remains in contact with the recording industry, his old friends seem to have abandoned him. At James's suggestion, Neil Young, David Crosby, Steven Stills, Stevie Wonder, Eddie Murphy, Smokey Robinson, and Teena Marie were all contacted for this story. None chose to comment.

James looks on the bright side. The current resurgence of 70s sounds and styles, "excites me, gives me lots of hope. Good old funk is back. People got to have it in their lives; there's too much thick shit out there. It's a relief. Reality sucks, and that's what they're selling today. There's too many rappers out there talking about death and Mac10s and all that shit. What happened to the fun, man? What happened to the funk?"

James insists, vehemently, that he wouldn't be in jail if "I wasn't black, if I wasn't who I am, if I didn't say what I was saying, if I didn't fuck so many white girls. Torturing a girl for stealing an eight-ball? *Shit.* There was probably a half pound of crumbs stuck in the carpet! Gimme a fuckin break. And the DA gives that bitch heroin to testify!"

He realizes, however, that he was bound for fall. He couldn't stop himself. Someone had to. These last two years in prison haven't been so bad, really. He's been reading a lot, finishing his book, his screenplays, writing new music on his guitar. In a way, he says, prison is the best thing that could have happened.

"It stopped me from doing drugs. It gave me a good chance to get clear. It gave me a chance to rest, to get my thoughts together, to eat three meals a day, to get healthy again. I see now that I can love again, that I can love me again. I'm not a has-been, and I'm not just a nobody. I'm not a cold-blooded maniacal killer, and I'm not a black Marquis de Sade.

"What I am is James Johnson, also known as Rick James, who happened to let his life run amok because of a fucking pipe and a rock of cocaine."

Upon James' release from Folsom in August 1996, after serving two years, he and Sager struck up a friendship on the outside. Many sushi dinners, most on Sunset Boulevard in Hollywood, were involved, and many tooth-grinding stories were exchanged. Another favorite hangout was Genghis Cohen, a kosher Chinese restaurant on Fairfax Avenue. For a time, James and Sager collaborated on a book proposal for a James autobiography, but a deal could not be struck, and the book was abandoned. As part of that process, Sager may or may not have taken a turn at the stove in an effort to best the legendary cooking efforts of James' former employee, Chef Boyardee.

After suffering a stroke and a hip replacement, James died on August 6, 2004. During his last years, James enjoyed a comeback of sorts initiated in great part by the groundbreaking comedy of David Chappell, who in a sketch coined the refrain: "I'm Rick James, bitch." James iconic music continued to be played all through his life and beyond his death, his estate presided over by his daughter Ty James.

In one of his last interviews, with the Atlanta Journal Constitution, James said he was reading Sager's bestselling collection, Scary Monsters and Super Freaks, "Because I'm in it, and because Mike wrote it, and Mike's a dear friend."

In an email to Sager the day after his death, a mutual friend, L.A. set designer Averie S., wrote:

"I was with Rick the night before he died and, believe it or not, he was singing your praises, showing your book to the other girl that was there. He went on and on about you for a very long time, talked about your experience in the crack house, etc., etc. The other girl and I were the last two to see him alive."

REQUIEM FOR A GANGSTA

Eric "Eazy E" Wright was a crack dealer who formed, along with icons Dr. Dre and Ice Cube, the seminal rap group Niggas Wit Attitude. Eazy's lifestyle set the bar for hip hop culture. But in the end, it wasn't guns or rivals that got him—shockingly, he succumbed to AIDS.

The bass beat faded, the video screen turned to snow. The CEO of Ruthless Records thumbed the remote, tilted back in his leather chair, adjusted his wraparound shades, inhaled deeply on a fragrant blunt. The next move was his.

He regarded the gentlemen before him, then regarded them some more. At 30, Eazy-E was the founder, owner and president, as well as chief executive, of Ruthless Records. He said sometimes that the *E* stood for Eric; his full name was Eric Wright. Other times he said it stood for Encino, though the significance of a nowhere valley town to a guy raised in Compton, the heart of gang turf in South Central Los Angeles, was left unexplained. He was also heard to declare, in his sly, trademark, high-pitched voice, that the *E* was for entrepreneur. Eazy was always angling to make money. As a kid, he bicycled a paper route, mowed lawns. Later he graduated to burglary, selling rock cocaine. For the past nine years, he'd been a music mogul.

Eazy figured the ends of his sparse mustache. It was a spring afternoon in 1994; his gold-and-diamond ID bracelet glowed in the midday light filtering through the tinted windows of his office suite. With his eyes shielded by dark green locs, his milk-chocolate face totally devoid of expression, you could never tell where you stood in negotiations with Eazy. He would read a magazine during a meeting, chew paper, toss spitballs. When you pitched him, you wound up and threw, then dangled there, hanging off balance at the edge of the mound, waiting for a call, waiting a little longer.

The Rise and Fall of a Super Freak

Eazy eyeballed the group fidgeting before him, some Mexican rappers called Brownside. He sucked his teeth. His Ebel watch ticked off the seconds.

What up with this nigga? wondered Toker, the leader of Brownside, seated at the moment across two long, black leather sofas. Toker, Danger, Trigga, Sharp, Junior, and Boxer were decked in full Mexican-gangsta regalia—neatly pressed Pendletons buttoned at the neck, white T-shirts beneath, khakis oversized enough to fold into pleats. Two of them wore hair nets, one a blue do-rag. Their gats were stashed outside, in the trunk of Toker's '64 Impala low-rider. The scent of pomade radiated around them, mingling in the air with Eazy's Jheri Kurl juice and the strong stink of indica bud.

Toker waited him out. He wasn't goin' to say squat. This was Eazy's hood, all uppity-uppity, a place called Woodland Hills, with huge cribs looking like Swiss chalets and mini-Tara and shit, lawns like a golf course. Though it was only ten or fifteen miles from where Toker grew up, he'd never heard of the place. Toker and them had rolled all the way here in the right lane of the freeway, worried about missing the exit.

Brownside was up from 49th Street, South Central L.A., Crip county. Back in the day, in the mid-'80s, when Toker was first on the corner, having turned from gangbanging to slinging rock cocaine, everybody had just started listening to rap. You had Ice-T trying to come out hard-core, but mostly there really wasn't nothing that nobody could relate to. They rhymes was wack.

Then Toker heard Eazy on the radio. He was kickin' songs about what was happening on the street: drive-bys, dope sacks, police wacks. It was what they was living.

Beginning in 1986, with the release of a twelve-inch single, "Boyz-n-the-Hood," and following up two years later with the album *Eazy-Duz-It*, by Eazy, and a year after that with *Straight Outta Compton*, by his seminal group, Niggaz Wit Attitude (N.W.A.), Eazy-E and Ruthless Records had pioneered what has come to be known as gangsta rap. Along the way, Eazy helped to remake the face of style, entertainment, and politics in America.

Like rock and roll in the '50s and soul in the '60s, gangsta rap has become the coin of the creative realm. The form can be seen in everything from the baggy look in fashion to the reality-oriented programming on television. Rap's content of discontent—sanctified by the Rodney King beating, by crime statistics, by a general foment among minorities of every stripe—has contributed to the embattlement of the proverbial "old white men in suits," an assault on the status quo in America that has translated into political upheaval and, recently, to direct attacks on rap by conservatives. To some, rappers like Eazy are the trumpeters of the apocalyptic hordes.

But to guys like Toker, to millions of kids across the country, Eazy's was the ultimate success story. He was an explorer who opened up new territory, created new possibilities. He defied the old rules, made up new ones as he went along. He did megabusiness with a joint between his lips. He released songs with titles like "Fuck tha Police." He made white people sweat. He giggled all the way to the bank.

Soon everyone in the ghetto was aspiring to rap stardom, buying drum machines and eight-track recorders, forming labels, rhyming about 9s and .40s and bitches and hoes. Then the folks in Hollywood discovered gangsta culture and the next thing you knew, white kids in Kansas were wearing falling-down jeans, greeting one another with a hearty "Yo!"

After a few years on the corner, Toker and his homies decided that there oughta be some Mexican rappers, too. They wrote a song called "Gang Related," bought time at a studio. They rented video cameras, hired some white guys to play cops. Then they hired a music lawyer who got them this meeting with Eazy-E.

Now, sitting expectantly on the leather sofas, Toker and his boyz continued to fidget. Eazy said nothing, just kicked it in his executive chair, his chin hiked, giving him the proud effect of a king. He pulled on his blunt—a short cigar hollowed of tobacco and refilled with weed. He adjusted his bracelet. He picked a piece of skin off one knuckle. He liked to keep his hands rough, he told people, in case he had to mix it up. For such a little man—five feet four, maybe 130 pounds—he did have big hands. How many fights he'd actually been in was subject to some question. But it didn't matter. What was strongest about Eazy was his bank. He always had a thick roll of dead presidents in his pocket. He paid for his Mercedes 600 SEL with cash. He told people his company was worth $20 million. His personal fortune, he said, was $60 million.

Finally, Eazy spoke. "Mannn," he said, shaking his head, his moist ringlets tickling the back of his neck. "This is like some cool shit here, man. Who owns you guys?"

"Don't nobody own us, motherfucker," said Toker.

"Who shot the video?" Eazy asked.

"We shot it ourself."

"Man, you bullshittin'," laughed Eazy, slapping his thigh. "Where you guys get the money?"

Toker eyeballed him. "Where you get *your* money when you started?"

Eazy regarded them a moment, refocusing. "*Daaamn!*" he exclaimed. "It's like that!"

"It's like that, *motherfucker*," declared Toker. He folded his arms across his chest, raised his own chin a notch.

"So what kinda deal you want?" asked Eazy. "What up, man? I wanna fuck with you guys. Let's do business."

"Look, homey," said Toker. "We don't want no money up front. We got our own label. All we lookin' for is a motherfucker who wants to fuck with us and give us some kind of distribution deal. We kinda want to get our foot in the door, man."

"Oh, man," said Eazy—a sudden, theatrical frown. "I don't think nobody gonna give you guys no deal like that."

Toker sagged. Back on 49th Street, he said something, and it happened. Here in Woodland Hills, his juice was water. He shrugged. "Well, look man," said Toker. "How would you come at us? That's why we came to you, man."

With that, Eazy giggled his smart-ass little giggle and signed yet another rap act. For no money down, on the strength of a handshake, Eazy picked up the option on Brownside's work, present and future, and the option of signing any other group that Toker and Fellon Records wanted to bring in.

In return, Brownside gained a place on an august family tree that had as its roots N.W.A.—featuring Ice Cube, Dr. Dre, and MC Ren. Its branches included the D.O.C., Michel'le, Above the Law, all the way up to Snoop Doggy Dogg, The Dogg Pound, Hoes With Attitude, Bone Thugs-N-Harmony.

That spring, as Toker and his homies sat before him, Eazy and Ruthless were as hot as a Tec-9 at a drive-by. He had more than thirty groups signed to his label. Demo tapes by the dozen were stashed in the trunk of his gray Mercedes, along with videos, clothing, and old containers of carryout food.

His *Ruthless Radio Show*, on KKBT-FM, in L.A., a Saturday-night call-in party show with Eazy on the mike, was being shopped nationally for syndication. A video game featuring Eazy's likeness was due out soon. His movie production company, Broken Chair Flickz, was circulating a screenplay around Hollywood. Another rap record company, catering to children, was also being discussed.

Eazy's recent EP, *It's On (Dr. Dre) 187um Killa*, had entered the R & B charts at number one. Sales had reached double platinum, 2 million—payback for the loss of face Eazy had suffered at the hands of his old discovery, Dr. Dre, and Dre's new manager, Suge Knight. A two-volume set was nearing completion. *Str.8 Off the Streetz of Muthaphukkin Compton* would feature collaborations with artists ranging from Guns N' Roses guitarist Slash to Naughty by Nature. Also in storage was enough never-before-released music by N.W.A. for a double album. Eazy's dream was a reunion of the group, most of whose members weren't speaking to him anymore. Though it didn't seem likely—they countered with talk of a reunion of N.W.E., "Niggaz Without Eazy"—he was still trying. He told people he'd find a way.

"Ninety-five gonna be our year, man," Eazy told Toker and Brownside, sitting on the sofa. "Ruthless gonna blow the fuck up!"

As it turned out, 1995 was Eazy-E's last year.

In February, after checking into L.A.'s Cedars-Sinai Medical Center with chest pains and breathing problems—he thought it was a lingering case of asthmatic bronchitis—Eazy learned he had AIDS.

He died a month later, on March 26, of heart failure due to a collapsed lung and AIDS-related pneumonia.

Ten days before his death, his attorney read a statement from Eazy, announcing his illness. The volume of sympathy calls from fans was such that Cedar-Sinai, a hospital long accustomed to celebrity patients, was forced to employ extra operators. Eazy received more calls at the hospital than Lucille Ball had.

Eazy left behind a wife, Tomica Woods, a former assistant at Motown, who declined to be interviewed for this article. Depending upon whom you believe, they'd been married in a hospital room either two days or three weeks before his death. The couple had a young son, Derrek, and a little girl, Daijah Nakia, who was born in September of '95. Tomica and son have so far tested negative for HIV. There are seven other acknowledged children, by six other women.

Also left behind was a new will, reams of litigation, mass confusion. Shortly after Eazy's death, police locked the doors of Ruthless Records to protect tapes and videos, which were beginning to disappear. A lawsuit by Michael Klein, director of business affairs for Ruthless Records, claims 50 percent ownership of Ruthless. The suit questions the validity of the will and of the marriage, which was performed either while Eazy was on heavy medication or the day before he was put on life-support systems. It asks for a determination of company ownership. The suit alleges that Eazy had often said he'd never marry, that in his "debilitated state" he'd been duped into the marriage and the new will. It also alleges that thousands had been diverted from Ruthless bank accounts by Tomica and her attorneys. At this writing, the court has appointed a special administrator to oversee operations at Ruthless Records.

Also before a court is a petition asking the hospital to turn over samples of Eazy's blood for a DNA test. At issue is the paternity of an infant, "Baby M." An attorney representing two other children has also filed a paternity suit. People close to Eazy expect many such suits. Wherever he went, women asked for his phone number. He took theirs instead, jotting them down in a small spiral notebook he always carried. It is said that he often had sex with five different women a day. He told folks he wanted a football team of kids. He lavished clothes and attention upon all his acknowledged children, sent them to expensive private schools, provided nice cars for the moms.

Eazy's death brought to a close what was arguably the most influential career in rap music to date. As of July 1994, the progeny of Eazy-E—rappers he discovered, rappers discovered by people he discovered—had sold more than 28 million albums. Today, with sales increasing exponentially from new groups and old titles, it is probably close to 50 million or more.

***

"Yo, listen up," said Eazy-E to the homeboys he had assembled, an all-star crew of young rappers standing around a glowing sound board. "What we need is some new shit. That other shit ain't sellin'."

"Well, what you lookin' for?" asked Dr. Dre.

"I don't know," said Eazy. "Something hard. Superhard. Maybe a lot of cussing."

The year was 1986. The place was Donavan Sound Studios, in Torrance. Eazy was 22, the oldest person in the room. A bright kid with loving parents—his mother a Montessori teacher, his father a Postal Service worker—he had turned inexplicably to the gang life. He had dropped out of school in tenth grade, proceeded to step up the ladder of crime.

By now he was rolling a burgundy Suzuki Samurai with a white top, wearing gold chains. How Eazy got the idea to become a rap mogul no one seems to remember, though he did like to go to the clubs and to the rap parties held regularly at Skateland and World on Wheels, near his neighborhood. Maybe in music and musicians he saw a potential for power similar to the kind he wielded in the world of drugs. He knew that dealing wouldn't last forever.

He called his company Ruthless Records, a reflection of his self-perceived style of business. He *was* pretty ruthless. Take the group gathered at Donovan Sound. He'd gone out and stolen them, raiding the best talent from an already existing label, Crew Cut Records, run by a guy named Lonzo. From the group CIA, he took Ice Cube, a young songwriting prodigy. From World Class Wreckin' Cru came DJ Yella and Dr. Dre.

Dre was the heavyweight on the scene at the time. He was a deejay at a popular club called Dotos. His group was one of L.A.'s first well-known rap acts. Its members wore glitter makeup and lacy clothes, aimed for dirty/funny in their rhymes. At Dre's suggestion, Eazy recruited MC Ren and Arabian Prince (who would later enter rap-trivia annals as the dropped sixth member of the original N.W.A.).

In the spring of '86, when Eazy put his group together at the studio, L.A. rap music was considered imitative and second-rate. The prevailing belief was that hard-edged urban rap could breed only under the close, foul-weather conditions of the East Coast ghetto. Though Ice-T and his crime raps were beginning to emerge, the most popular California acts were jesters like Tone Loc and the L.A. Dream Team. "Our music is different from the East Coast," said one of the Dream Team. "It's more musical, more up-tempo. It's not as hard a life. We do have street violence, but the New York life is harder than that of sunny California and Hollywood."

And so it was that Eazy rented this studio and assembled his little Manhattan Project of rap. After much debate, the time ticking away, Eazy suggested that Cube write about gangs, the whole lifestyle Eazy had been living. They came up with "Boyz-n-the-Hood."

They laid the tracks, Eazy doing most of the rapping. Eazy took the tape to Macola Records, a custom pressing plant on Santa Monica Boulevard. For $7,000 in cash, Eazy got 10,000 twelve-inch vinyl records. He drove them to stores, sold them to dealers at swap-meets. He ordered more. By word of mouth alone, the record sold 500,000 copies.

In March of 1987, Eazy met Jerry Heller in the lobby of Macola. Heller had started with promoter Bill Graham at the beginning of the rock era. Heller had been the first to bring Elton John and Pink Floyd to America. Legendary music manager Irving Azoff called Heller his mentor. Heller thought Ruthless was the greatest name for a record company he'd ever heard. Knowing the formula for musical success—the more hated by parents, the more popular with the kids—Heller recognized rap as the next wave.

After playing the demo for a few of his old contacts, who told him he was crazy, Heller went to Priority Records. Priority's marquee act was the California Raisins. The deal Heller cut at Eazy's insistence was unique. All records would be released by the Ruthless label, through Eazy's production company, a privilege and a piece of the action that was usually reserved for only the biggest stars.

In September 1988, Eazy and his group once again went into the studio. When *Straight Outta Compton* was released by Niggaz Wit Attitude, featuring its keynote song, "Fuck tha Police," a firestorm erupted. Radio stations and MTV refused to play the cut. The album went gold in weeks.

In Phoenix, midway through a fifty-city tour, things began to go south for N.W.A. The members of the group were feuding with Eazy, questioning their shares of royalties and gate receipts. Eazy gave Jerry Heller a call, and Heller flew down with dubious contracts for all the members to sign, plus signing bonuses of $75,000 each. "He said, 'If you sign the contract, you get the check,'" Ice Cube recalled in a 1990 interview.

"So, Heller give me this contract, and I said I wanted a lawyer to see it. Everybody else signed," said Cube. "I just told them, 'I wanna make sure my shit right first.' I remember them niggas jokin'. They say, 'Yo! $75,000! If that shit ain't right, ain't nothin' right!'"

In the end, Cube left the group. Eazy-E kept silent, let Heller speak for him. "The real reason Ice Cube left N.W.A. was that he was incredibly jealous of the notoriety and success of Eazy-E," Heller has said. "He wanted to be Eazy-E. He was jealous because not only is Eazy a key member of N.W.A. with a successful solo career, he's also the president of his own record company. Eazy-E is a major star and a successful businessman. Ice Cube isn't."

"How can I be jealous of a motherfucker with no talent?" asked Cube in response. "He got money. I'm gonna have talent and money."

N.W.A.'s third album, *Efil4zaggin* ("Niggaz 4 Life" spelled backward), was made without him. It was the first gangsta-rap album to reach number one on *Billboard's* chart.

Cube went on to a successful solo career. Soon he debuted as an actor, later as a producer. His first role was in the movie *Boyz N the Hood*.

***

Eazy-E stared up at the man before him, a guy they called Suge (pronounced Shug, as in sugar). Six feet three, 320 pounds, a former football star turned bodyguard turned rap manager, Marion "Suge" Knight had a reputation for violence. In the near future, he would be sued by two rappers charging assault. The rappers, two brothers, would allege that Suge pulled a gun, hit one of them on the head with it, forced them both to remove their clothes, then robbed them. Suge was Dr. Dre's new manager. (Knight declined to be interviewed for this article.)

"Where Dre at?" asked Eazy, trying to sound tough. It was an evening in April 1991, at a darkened sound studio at Solar Records. Dre had paged Eazy, asking for a meeting, one-on-one. Now Dre was nowhere to be found.

"We don't need him for this piece of business," said Suge, reaching for his breast pocket. He pulled out some legal documents.

For months, according to a suit filed under federal racketeering statutes in Los Angeles federal court, Suge Knight and his posse had been terrorizing Ruthless Records. It had begun more than a year earlier, when Dr. Dre and Eazy had a falling out, and Dre signed with Suge. Together they formed their own company, Death Row Records.

Known by now as the best producer in the business, Dre took with him the top acts from the Ruthless stable—Michel'le, Kokane, D.O.C. Just as Eazy had robbed Lonzo at Crew Cut Records, Suge and Dre had now ganked Eazy. This time, however, there was a slight problem. The rap business had become more sophisticated. A victor could no longer just take the spoils. He needed a signed, notarized release.

When Eazy refused to release Dre and the others, Suge began a reign of terror. One day, according to court documents, Suge walked straight into Jerry Heller's office at Ruthless and placed his index finger on Heller's gray temple. "I could have blown you away right now," he was alleged to have said.

Heller hired an Israeli security consultant and two bodyguards; he installed surveillance cameras and extra alarms. He ordered that a shotgun be kept under the reception desk at Ruthless. He kept guns in every room of his house, a grand stucco affair in a gated community in Calabasas, two doors down from Eazy. Dre lived one block over.

Eazy fronted off the threats, kept on the move. He had always spent most of his time in his cars anyway. He'd drive around all night thinking, making calls, visiting women. Eazy liked his women short and pretty, feisty, sort of street but with some education.

He wore two pagers on his belt, kept three cellular phones within reach. He seldom drank, though at a nice club he'd order a Midori sour. He liked eating at McDonald's, Benihana, Sizzler, or anywhere he could get his favorite dish, fettuccine Alfredo. He often ordered several entrees to pick through. He loved Disney World, other theme parks with rides; he loved visiting his children, though he usually didn't stay long. It seemed like he always had a meeting to make, some work to do, Monday through Sunday, 24-7. He'd show up at Jerry Heller's house at three in the morning with a demo tape someone had handed him in a club.

Eazy rarely stayed in his own lavish house in Calabasas. Having grown up in the friendly, cacophonous atmosphere of the hood, Eazy thought the house, secreted in a canyon a few miles from Malibu, surrounded by rich white people, was isolated and creepy, too quiet. He also had a big house in Westlake with a waterfall out back. He hardly ever went there either. He preferred his house in Norwalk, a short drive from Compton.

The Calabasas house was even bigger and farther away than the Westlake place. In the white marble foyer, there was a neon sign, WELCOME TO EAZY'S PLAYHOUSE. It was a great party house, and that's what he used it for. You'd walk in and find three or four kinds of designer marijuana on the dining room table, plenty of beer and juice and whatnot in the fridge. The living room was done in white shag carpet with cream-colored leather couches, brass-and-glass tables. A huge entertainment room was painted completely black. It sported a projection TV and a state-of-the-art audio system. Scattered around the house were his various collections: pogues, pistols, bottles of designer cologne. His other passion was expensive monster dolls—Freddy Krueger, a $2,500 Chucky. Most of the dolls came from kits, which Eazy paid people to assemble.

The big garages at the houses also served him well. Besides the gray Mercedes, Eazy had a Jeep Cherokee, a couple of BMWs. He owned four vintage Impala low-riders—three from 1964, one from 1963. The cars were stacked: Dayton wide wheels, full hydraulics that could bounce the cars off the pavement like basketballs. The stereo systems ran $15,000.

Now, however, in a darkened sound studio, Eazy was on foot and alone. His best producer and former best friend had left his company, taking with him Ruthless's biggest acts. Suge Knight loomed above him, brandishing legal papers releasing Eazy's artists.

"So, you gonna sign the releases?" asked Suge, according to court documents.

"Fuck you, motherfucker," said Eazy.

"Look G," Suge allegedly said. "I got Jerry Heller stashed in a van."

"Fuck you!" said Eazy.

Then Suge pulled another piece of paper from a pocket, a wrinkled scrap. On it was written an address in Compton. "I know where you mamma stay," said Suge, nodding his head toward a dark corner of the room. Two bodyguards stepped forward, each carrying a lead pipe.

Eazy signed the releases.

Dr. Dre's first album with Death Row Records, *The Chronic*, was released in 1992. The video for the single "Dre Day" went into heavy rotation on MTV. The guest rapper on the cut was Dre's new discovery, Snoop Doggy Dogg. The video featured an Eazy-E look-alike jumping up and down like a clown. Behind him was a group of rappers portraying minstrel-show types. A pudgy, gray-haired white guy ordered them around. "I work fro Sleazy E—I wouldn't have it any other way," the white guy declared, winking. "Just sign your life—I mean your name—on the contract."

The song ended like this: "Oh yeah. And P.S. Fuck Mr. Roarke and Tattoo, a.k.a. Jerry and Eazy."

The record sold 3 million.

Eazy collected a percentage of the royalties, a condition of the contract that Knight and Dre eventually signed in order to legally release Dre's album.

Says a record promoter who worked with Eazy since the Macola days: "I think Suge kinda stole a lot of Eazy's self-esteem, you know, bum-rushin' his office, taking away his groups. Then Dre come out dissin' him on MTV. Daaamn! Suge kinda made him a broken man. Eazy lost a lot of respect behind that. No matter how many lawyers and managers you got, rap is still a contact sport, you know what I'm sayin'? People thought Eazy come off with his tail between his legs like a bitch."

***

"What did the doctor say?" asked Eazy from his hospital bed in Cedars-Sinai. "What did they tell you?"

"Ummm, he said your T-cells are kind of low, and that those are the good ones that fight off the virus and stuff," said Charis Henry, Eazy's former assistant, a homegirl and ex-rapper with a degree from Loyola Marymount.

When Eazy dropped all that weight, then ended up in the hospital, Charis put two and two together and rushed to his side. She had started working for Eazy at her own suggestion. Over the years, they'd become close, but they were never lovers. She knew a different Eazy: boyish, silly, sly, mindful of his language. He always excused himself when he cursed in front of her.

Charis had been with Eazy since before the falling-out with Dre. She was the one who had written the $2,500 check that bought Eazy his seat at a luncheon in Washington, D.C., with 1,400 Republicans and President George Bush, a little joke Eazy played on the White Establishment after he'd found himself on a Republican fund-raising list.

Charis was the one who called up the lawyers when Eazy wanted to get in touch with L.A. police officer Theodore Briseno, one of the defendants in the Rodney King beating. Eazy attended the trial almost daily, sitting near Briseno. He told the press that Briseno was a Mexican, not a white guy. He said Briseno had tried to stop the beating. Other rappers said Eazy was a sellout, raising the puppet theme once again.

Charis had also been there as Eazy slowly recovered from his loss of face at the hands of Suge and Dr. Dre. Soon after the alleged reign of terror abated—an easing of hostilities that coincided with the filing of the federal racketeering charges against Suge Knight—Eazy began working even harder than before, signing groups, releasing albums, coming up with new ideas. With the release of *It's On (Dr. Dre) 187um Killa*, Eazy was clearly back in the house. "'Dre Day' was my payday, and Snoop look like an anorectic mutt," Eazy rapped, a dis that made people stand up and go "Daaamn!" Eazy had fought back to respectability.

Recently (under Tomica's influence, many say), Eazy had parted ways with Jerry Heller and with Priority Records. With Heller out of the way, rumors went, chances for an N.W.A. reunion seemed brighter. Eazy was photographed talking with Ice Cube at a New York club, their first major conversation since the Phoenix incident nine years earlier.

Now, in a private hospital room filled with flowers, Charis was trying to put a positive spin on some bad news, chattering nonstop like always. What the doctor had said, precisely, was that Eazy's T-cell count was only five. Charis and Tomica, also present in the room on this March afternoon, had decided that it wasn't necessary to tell him the exact number.

"So, what we need to do is build those T-cells up," Charis continued cheerfully. "There's teas and things you can take. Don't worry about that. But right now, I want you to continue eating. If you have four bites of fruit today, I want you to have eight tomorrow. If you don't eat—"

Eazy cut his eyes to Charis. He looked annoyed.

"Do you want me to leave?" Charis asked Eazy.

"No," said Eazy, his voice muffled under an oxygen mask. "I want you to be quiet."

"Well, I'll tell you what," said Charis. "You eat five bites of soup, and I'll be quiet."

Eazy perked up, pulled the mask off his face. "Hurry up and give me the soup," he said with a smirk.

***

They buried Eazy-E in a gold-plated coffin, wearing baggy jeans, a Pendleton shirt, wraparound shades, a Compton hat. Missing from his outfit were his gold-and-diamond bracelet, his Ebel watch, his assortment of gold rings. He lay in state, fingers interlaced, at the foot of the altar in the massive sanctuary of the First African Methodist Episcopal Church, a stately brick monolith with stained-glass windows on a little hill overlooking deepest South Central. Outside, police patrolled every corner for miles. People made their way quietly, reverently, by car and on foot, toward the church from every direction.

As bow-tied Fruit of Islam bodyguards watched closely, more than 3,000 mourners filed past Eazy's body: teenagers and church ladies, homeboys, club girls and neighborhood folk, a number of white record execs, even the mayor of Compton. The city council had proclaimed this Eazy-E Day. For better and for worse, Eazy had put Compton on the world map.

Ten days before he died, Eric "Eazy-E" Wright issued this statement:

I may not seem like a guy that you'd pick to preach a sermon, but I feel it's now time to "testify" because I do have folks that care about me hearing all kinds of stories about what's up.

Yeah, I was a brother on the streets of Compton doing a lot of things most people look down on, but it did pay off. Then, we started rapping about real stuff that shook up the LAPD and the FBI, but we got our message across big-time and everyone in America started paying attention to the boyz in the hood. Soon our anger and hopes got everyone riled up.

There were great rewards for me personally like fancy cars, gorgeous women, and good livin'. Like real non-stop excitement. I'm not religious but wrong or right, that's me. I'm not saying this because I'm looking for a soft cushion wherever I'm heading, I just feel that I've got thousands and thousands of young fans that have to learn about what's real when it comes to AIDS. . . . I would like to turn my own problem into something good that will reach out to all my homeboys and their kin because I want to save their asses before it's too late.

*"Requiem for a Gangsta" received ASCAP's 1996 Deems Taylor Award for Distinguished Music Writing.

"DAMN! THEY GONNA LYNCH US!"

Black motorist Rodney Glenn King's videotaped beating, at the hands of the Los Angeles Police Department, would eventually touch off massive riots. A look at what happened that fateful night, from both inside and outside of King's vehicle.

Pooh and Glenn and Freddie G. was kickin' it late that night outside Pooh's house, all three sitting in the car. The stars were out, and the radio hummed blues into the cool March air. It was a typical Saturday on the wrong side of Altadena, near the border between the Bloods and the Crips; some homeboys, some reefer, some Old English 800, something ready to go down.

Glenn was behind the wheel of the white Hyundai, a four-door that belonged to his grandma. He stared out the windshield, worrying his sparse mustache. Freddie G. snored at shotgun, his crippled leg snug in a metal brace. Pooh lounged behind Glenn, lids heavy, head angled forward to keep his Jheri curl from getting scrunched. It had been a long night. Sort of a reunion.

Glenn had been trying to hook up with Pooh all week. Tonight, he'd just come on by the house. Pooh was playing with his baby girl, half-watching television.

"What up?" said Glenn. He'd walked over, slid Pooh some skin. He'd known Pooh since Little League. Through the years, they'd lost touch on and off, but that's how it was in the neighborhood. You away a while, you back, you pick right up. Glenn was chatty, like always, pretty funny, built like Baby Huey, six feet three. He liked Snickers bars, Mexican food, Marlboros in a box, the ladies. Twenty-five years old, he was married to his second wife, Crystal. She had two kids. They lived with his relatives in the house where he grew up.

Pooh and Glenn had chilled a while, then hooked up with Freddie G. Helms and drove to the park. Then they rode back to Pooh's house, parked by the curb. Freddie G. rapped a little, fell asleep. Now it was quiet in the car, just the music from the radio, a show called *The Quiet Storm*. Then Glenn started the car and drove off down the hill toward the Foothill Freeway, the 210.

Five hundred miles of freeway in Los Angeles County, a vast sprawling valley of highways, a canopy of stars and darkness, the mountains hunkered just north. A few dollars' worth in the tank, some homeys in the car, a pleasure cruise in a rolling clubhouse—what else is there to do? No apartment, no money, the movie stars got all the Lakers tickets. Concerts are too dangerous. House parties are okay, but you don't go unless it's people you deal with. You never know when you're gonna get caught in someone else's beef, settled with a spray of bullets.

They go to different cities—Monrovia, Duarte, Irvin, Pomona—different patches in the vast racial quilt that covers the San Fernando Valley, over the hill from Hollywood: cookie-cutter residential outposts of strip malls and fast-food joints. In some cities, all the signs are written in Chinese, all the cars are filled with Chinese people. In others, there are Vietnamese, Mexicans, Koreans, Salvadorans, blacks. White people are seen on occasion. Usually they're in black-and-white cars. On the doors, there's a sign written in English, the slogan of the Los Angeles Police Department: "TO PROTECT AND TO SERVE."

So that's what you do on a Saturday evening: Just get out on the freeway, choose an exit, turn right, right again, look around for ladies. Don't stay too long, though: too risky. At home in Altadena, the police get used to you. They don't mess with you if you ain't done nothing wrong. But if you go to a different city, they pull you over just like that, especially if there's a lot of guys with baseball caps in the car. They keep you ten or fifteen minutes. They ask what's going on in the neighborhood. You're like, "I don't know," 'cause you don't stay in that neighborhood. They make you sit on the curb or get down on your stomach. They put their knee in your back. They take your ID and forget to return it. Like Glenn once said, "They consider themselves different humans than we are. They all a family, one big family. And we another family."

The other choice is staying home, but Altadena's no picnic either, not on this side of town. East of Fair Oaks Avenue, that's chamber-of-commerce Altadena: million-dollar houses, Neighborhood Watch, the hundred-year-old deodar pines on Christmas Tree Lane festooned with holiday lights. West of Fair Oaks, down Lincoln Avenue, that's Pooh and Glenn and Freddie G.'s Altadena: cracking paint, brown weeds on the lawn, cars on cinder blocks in driveways, blue collars, brown skins, bandannas, suburban gangs.

Living as he did by the shifting border, Pooh had his days as a Blood. His set was the Playboys. His court file begins at age 15. Bryant Keith Allen, a.k.a. Pooh and Boss, was first arrested for stabbing a man in the stomach. He was sentenced to one year probation, 120 hours of community service. Two years later, he was arrested for swinging a blackjack at a man who was helping children board a school bus. Six months in probation camp, an A.A. meeting once a week. Returning home, Pooh was arrested for staggering along a street, a bottle of beer in his hand. Fifty more hours of community service.

Pooh went down hard two years later, when he was 19. At 8:15 one evening, Pooh and two accomplices, all of them armed with automatic pistols, robbed a liquor store. Two hours later, they hit a McDonald's. They roughed up the cashiers, brained the manager, emptied the cash drawers and the safe. Making their getaway, they encountered cops, who opened fire. Pooh went down, three shotgun pellets embedded in his leg and foot. He gave himself up.

Court records say that Pooh was suspected of pulling three to five other armed robberies that same month. His sentencing report recommended the max: "It seems the defendant is out of control and needs to be removed from society for the protection of us all." Pooh pleaded guilty, got five years.

Back on the block, Pooh was keeping clear, trying to put the gangs behind him. Recently, he'd ended the longest work stint of his life, six months with a paper company at $5.50 an hour.

Now Glenn nosed the Hyundai onto the entrance ramp of the 210. He stared straight ahead, hummed a song to himself. It was a simple life he'd led. His parents were Jehovah's Witnesses. His father was a handyman; on weekends he liked to fish and to drink whiskey. Glenn was in the special-education class in high school. He had trouble reading, often skipped school. By the time his class got to its senior year, Glenn was at least a grade behind. Six months before graduation, he dropped out. After that, Glenn seemed adrift. He was into singing on the corner, hanging out in the park.

Rodney Glenn King entered the system when he was 18, when he was arrested for trying to run down his first wife, Denetta. She chose not to press charges, and Glenn was convicted of reckless driving, sentenced to eighty-four hours of community service. Two months later, Glenn was arrested for stealing $251-worth of auto parts from the Pep Boys in Pasadena. He was found guilty of trespassing, placed on sixty days probation. In 1987, Glenn tried once again to run down Denetta. Once again, she chose not to press charges. Glenn pleaded no contest to misdemeanor battery and was placed in a domestic-violence program. Two years later, he was arrested for soliciting an undercover policewoman. Glenn pleaded guilty and was fined $352.50. When the fine went unpaid, an arrest warrant was issued. Tonight, it remained outstanding.

Glenn's one attempt at a capital crime was a stupendous failure. He was 23, by then divorced from Denetta and married to Crystal, a high-school friend. According to court records, early one evening Glenn got in the Hyundai and drove east, to a Chinese neighborhood called Monterey Park. He entered the 99 Market, bought a single piece of bubble gum, then pulled a two-foot tire iron from beneath his jacket. "Open the cash register," demanded Glenn, who loomed a foot taller than the store owner behind the counter, Tae Suck Baik.

Baik opened up, let Glenn take the cash. Then Glenn reached for two cashier's checks. Baik grabbed Glenn's hand. "You don't need checks," he said.

Glenn stopped a moment, pondering.

Baik reached below the counter, came up with a three-foot metal rod. He grabbed Glenn's jacket and began whipping him with the rod. Glenn staggered, fell, dropped his tire iron. Baik ran around the counter and hit Glenn some more. Glenn reached for an aluminum pole, hit Baik once, then fled the scene with $200 and the cashier's checks. Baik ran out after him and wrote down the license number of the white Hyundai.

Ten days later, Glenn was apprehended, the checks still in his glove compartment. He was sentenced to two years in state prison. Released after one, he returned in December 1990 and went to work renovating concession stands at Dodger Stadium. "He never missed a day, including two weeks when he had car trouble and had to ride the bus from Chinatown and then walk over the bridge to the stadium," says his supervisor. "He was a good man. I think he was sorry when the job ended."

Now, at thirty minutes past midnight, Sunday, March 3, 1991, Glenn followed 210 as it banked gently west, a dark ribbon of asphalt cut through a fairy kingdom of textured hills and craggy mountains. He drove on, hypnotized by the series of glowing lane dots, by his thoughts. Freddie G. was still asleep. Pooh listened to the radio, a station called KKBT-FM, the Beat.

Past Pennsylvania Avenue, past La Tuna Canyon Road, past Sunland Avenue, past a California Highway Patrol car idling by the side of the road....

Inside the cop car, the radar gun shrieked. The deputies were a husband-and-wife team. T.J. and Melanie Singer. Startled, they checked the readout. One hundred and fifteen miles an hour, according to the report they filed later. The Hyundai whooshed past. The Singers peeled out, officers in hot pursuit, Code 2.

Pooh, in the backseat with his eyes closed, all of a sudden felt a little twinge, the kind you feel at a stoplight when someone's staring at you. He opened his eyelids to slits. Red light danced across the seat in front of him. He twisted around, head low, looked out the rear window.

Shit! Police!

Pooh turned toward the front. Freddie G. was still sleeping, Glenn drove on, seemingly unaware of the cops following them.

Why ain't Glenn pulling over? wondered Pooh.

***

Not far away, in a LAPD patrol car, a bulletin blipped across a computer screen. The terminal was mounted on a dashboard between the two officers. The Mobile Digital Terminal looks like a word processor. It is the latest hardware in the modern war on crime, linked by computer relay to the police department's NASA-developed command-and-control center, located in downtown L.A., five floors below ground in a hardened bunker.

It was against policy to send personal messages via the MDT, but on this night, Officer Larry Powell, riding with his partner, Timothy Wind, was taking the liberty to chitchat.

"What are you up to?" typed Officer Corina Smith. She and Powell were dating. "We are up on the rock on top of some abandoned house with narco and BFMV [burglary from a motor vehicle] suspects in it. We are waiting for them to hit some places."

"Sounds almost like our last call," typed Powell. "It was right out of Gorillas in the Mist."

"HaHaHaHa," typed Smith. "Let me guess who be the parties."

"Good guess," responded Powell.

Powell, 28, looked like a cop on the beat, pug-nosed and thick-jowled, Irish worry knitting his brow, he was a three-year veteran. His father, Edwin, was a Los Angeles County marshal. Former neighbors remember the boy as quiet, hardworking, responsible. If you ever needed a hand, you could ask him. After high school, Larry went to Cal State for two years, then joined the force. With their youngest gone, his mother and father had opened their empty nest to a series of babies born to drug-addicted mothers.

Before going on patrol tonight, Powell and other officers had trained with their PR-24 batons, two-foot metal-alloy nightsticks. Powell was judged weak and ineffective, ordered to drill a second time, concentrating on baton chops to the shoulder blades, elbows, wrists, knees, and ankles.

Powell's partner was a 30-year-old rookie who had graduated from the academy in November. He too had taken training tonight, to far better reviews. "He demonstrated excellent technique and made contact in all the right places on the practice board," his supervisor had noted.

Tall and skinny, with an overbite, Tim Wind had come to Foothill Division from Shawnee, Kansas, where he'd served on the fifty-four-member force in the suburb of Kansas City. Wind was married, the father of a toddler son. He was still on department probation.

Wind's move from Kansas was the law-enforcement opportunity of a lifetime. The LAPD, most cops will agree, is the nation's showcase force. Starting with *Dragnet, The Mod Squad, Adam-12,* and *S.W.A.T.*, up through *21 Jump Street*, fact and fantasy had begun to blur where California cops were concerned. The 8,300 very real men and women of the LAPD had become something of a legend, their chief looked upon as kind of a four-star general of local crime fighting. The LAPD had a reputation as being a closed society—a clean-cut, paramilitary organization that dealt in only the finest: training, equipment, commanders, men.

Just then, at 12:47 a.m., a message from headquarters interrupted Smith and Powell: "To all units: CHP advises their officers are in pursuit of a vehicle failing to yield, white Hyundai, license 2KFM102, now approaching Glenoaks. . . ."

Powell and Wind took off.

Back in the Hyundai, Pooh swiveled, checked the rear. The police were gaining. Why Glenn acting like this? he wondered. To Pooh, Glenn was usually one of the smart ones. He wasn't no gang banger; he was always the one sayin' you shouldn't do this or that. But now Glenn was behind the wheel, and it was like he wasn't there. Who knows where he was? Maybe thinking about getting caught and violating his parole. Maybe thinking about that old bench warrant; the cops could take him right off the street. Maybe, says a friend, Glenn was off in a faraway place he sometimes goes. It's a defense mechanism or something, an escape route. Just now, with the police in pursuit, it was as if he'd had a glitch. Something in his brain that said, This isn't really happening. It's gonna go away.

Glenn pulled off the freeway at the Paxton Street exit and rolled through a stop sign at the bottom of the off-ramp at about fifty miles per hour, according to police.

Pooh was getting scared. The cops were closing in. Glenn stopped for a red light, then gassed it. Sirens now, more cars, Powell and Wind, others, Code 3. A helicopter beat the air overhead. Pooh thought to himself, The next stop that come, I'm gonna jump out the car! Then he thought better: No, I can't do that. The police might think I got something. Then he realized: Shit! These motherfuckers could start shooting!

Pooh swiveled, raised his palms high, surrendering out the rear window. "Glenn! Glenn!" he hollered. "Pull over! Stop!"

***

Fifty years ago, had there been a balcony where George Holliday's now stands, the view of Hansen Dam would have been breathtaking. Shimmering in the undulating foothills, Holiday Lake stretched 130 blue acres, 30 feet deep, a huge park built by the county in 1949. Rimmed with trucked-in sand, there was a shallow section for swimmers, barbecue pits on a wide grassy knoll for lazy Sunday afternoons. On weekends, the parking lot was jammed with colorful cars with big metal fins, filled with postwar Americans hard at work developing the concept of leisure time.

Years went by. Heavy rains and forest fires caused erosion, and silt from the San Gabriel Mountains and the Angeles Forest filled the lake. By 1982, the water was declared stagnant and unhealthy. Today, heavy machinery rumbles in a big pit, scooping up the 30 million tons of rock and sand and silt in what was once Holiday Lake. Homeless men wander the hills, picking through dumpsters. The parking lot is now a city street, a scene out of urban South Central, plucked up somehow by Providence and landed amid green landscape. Black men stand in clusters, drinking from paper cups; money and drugs change hands. Two rusty motor homes are parked semi-permanently. People knock, enter, the doors bang shut.

Though the lake died a premature death, the Foothill District, as it is known to the LAPD, would begin to flourish. In the past ten years, due mostly to Asian and Hispanic immigration, California's population has grown twice as fast as the rest of the country's. Foothill has absorbed much of the new burden: Nestled into the mountains, twenty minutes from downtown, it is the fastest-growing community in L. A. County.

Sixty percent Hispanic, ten percent black, thirty percent Asian and Anglo, as Caucasians have come to be termed on the California census, it is a demographic picture of America's future. The area is plagued with the most drunk drivers, heroin addicts, and car thefts in the San Fernando Valley, a bubbling pepper pot of towns and colors and trouble.

The statistics don't lie, but they don't tell the whole truth about Foothill, either. If you're not a person of color, if you're not poor or illiterate or unemployed, if you don't know anybody who breaks any laws, Foothill is a middle-class exurbia. Affordable condos, picket fences—this is the place where George Holliday moved three years ago, a pit stop on the road to what people used to know as the American Dream.

Born in Toronto, George lived most of his life in Indonesia and Argentina. Six years ago, at 26, he decided to come to America. George arrived at LAX with $700 in his pocket and a suitcase in each hand, a strapping, freckled, sandy-haired rugby player with an itch to succeed. By lunchtime the next day, he was cooking burgers in a fast-food place. He worked there for about two weeks, until he found a job as a plumber.

Today, George is the general manager of a local office of a national plumbing concern called Rescue Rooter. He recently married his Argentine girlfriend, Eugenia. They'd moved to Mountainback three years ago, a tidy development of neo-Tudor garden apartments, up a hill and behind an iron fence from Foothill Boulevard.

When they first had moved in, the neighborhood wasn't great. It seemed that every day, park rangers and police were rounding up drug dealers across the street at Hansen Dam. It was a bit of a nuisance and a little scary, considering the way they talked about it so much on the news. But when you came right down to it, none of it really touched George and Eugenia. "The cops, you're not really aware of them," says George. "You need them, you call them. The rest of the time you live your life."

And a good life it was. George had his work, Eugenia stayed home, met him often for lunch. A few months before, the couple had decided to buy a camcorder. George brought it home on Valentine's Day, a Sony CCD-F77. On Saturday night, March 2, George loaded film into the camera, plugged the battery pack into the recharger. The next day was the Los Angeles Marathon. He was sponsoring one of his employees in the race. He went to bed early, setting his alarm for 6 a.m.

Over the years, George had become accustomed to the night sounds of police sirens screaming down Foothill Boulevard. Usually, he slept right through it. But this night, at about 12:50 a.m., George woke with a start. Something was peculiar. The sirens wailed in the distance, as always, but this time they crescendoed and died with a screech of rubber outside his bedroom window. George jumped up, naked, from the bed and pulled back the window shade.

Across the boulevard, a hundred yards away, a white Hyundai was pulling to the curb. A half-dozen police cars pulled up around it.

George watched a second, then flashed. Hey, he thought, let's get the camera!

***

"DRIVER! PUT YOUR HANDS OUT THE WINDOW. TAKE YOUR LEFT HAND, UNLOCK THE DOOR, AND STEP OUT!"

Inside the white Hyundai, Freddie G. awoke with a start. When last he'd been conscious, he was chillin' in the car outside Pooh's house, in Altadena. Pooh, in the back, had his hands up, palms high in surrender. Glenn, legally drunk, struggled to execute the commands issuing from the PA. He blinked his eyes, tried to focus. He took his left hand off the steering wheel, rolled down the window, stuck his arm out. Then he took his right hand off the wheel. He reached across his chest.

Pooh peered out into the darkness. There was a grassy knoll, some high trees, white police everywhere. *Damn!* he thought. *They gonna lynch us or something.*

***

If you're black or brown or yellow and you live in Los Angeles in the year 1991, there are some things you just know. One is that two thirds of the county's population are people of color like you, and that the rest of the United States' cities are headed quickly in that direction. Another thing is this: white people are still in charge, and they generally make that clear.

How differently the police can be perceived:

"They consider themselves different humans than we are," Rodney Glenn King had said. "They all a family, one big family. And we another family."

"The cops, you're not really aware of them," George Holliday had said. "You need them, you call them. The rest of the time you live your life."

"There has existed for many years a simmering—something boiling—relationship of mistrust and animosity between the LAPD and Los Angeles's minority communities," the Southern California Chapter of the American Civil Liberties Union said recently. "This is fueled and maintained by abuse directed toward those communities [by the police] . . . who have shown a historic tolerance toward prejudice and abusive behavior within its own ranks."

In 1980, Los Angeles paid out slightly less than $1 million to resolve lawsuits alleging police misconduct. In 1989, the outlays had risen to $9.1 million. Last year, a record $11.3 million was paid to victims and families, more than in any other city in the nation except Detroit, which has 4,000 fewer officers than the LAPD.

The 1990 totals include suits alleging excessive force, false arrests, wrongful deaths, civil-rights violations, negligence, misconduct. Of the thirty-two cases settled, eight involved police shootings, thirteen involved physical abuse. Between 1987 and 1990, 4,400 misconduct complaints were filed against the LAPD. Forty-one percent of all complaints were filed by blacks, who comprise only 13 percent of the population of L.A.

In one case, police in an armored personnel carrier, mounted with a fourteen-foot battering ram, stormed a suspected crack house. Inside were three small children, two eating ice cream cones. No drugs were found. In a raid on a South Central neighborhood, a force of eighty LAPD officers beat and terrorized occupants of several apartments during a drug search, carried out with crowbars, sledgehammers, and axes. Several dozen suspected gang members were taken into custody, seven were booked—none was charged with a crime. In the aftermath, residents of the apartments discovered that one of the cops had spray-painted some graffiti on a living-room wall: "GANG TASK FORCE RULES!"

"There is a culture of violence that has swept the nation's police forces," said Representative John Conyers, of Michigan, a member of the Congressional Black Caucus. Analysts say police brutality has its roots in racism, academy training, group identification, slack departmental discipline, fraternal traditions that encourage a "code of silence" among officers. Police themselves say that they have been conditioned by experience to expect the worst in encounters with the public. "We've seen over and over how seemingly benign situations can result in our own deaths," wrote a female LAPD officer in a *Newsweek* editorial that ran on March 25. "The social conditions within which we operate are complex. So are the range of emotions each cop experiences daily. We never know what to expect. We all want to see tomorrow."

The roots of the LAPD's brutal statistics can be traced to its history. Back in the Twenties, when gangsters and vice lords were hip-deep in politics, the LAPD was known as the palace guard of the city bosses. In 1950, a reform movement was mounted, and the city charter was amended. New rules called for the chief of police to be hired through a civil-service process instead of being appointed by the mayor. The first new man was William H. Parker.

Next to FBI Director J. Edgar Hoover, Parker would become the most celebrated law-enforcement official in history. A former marine, Parker installed a boot camp and stressed chain of command and pride in badge and uniform. It was Parker who coined the phrase "thin blue line" to describe his police force, but he is best remembered for the inauguration of "proactive," offensive policing. Rather than wait for crime to be committed, Parker decided, the police should take the initiative: Go get them before they get us.

Parker's chauffeur and bodyguard back then was a young cop named Daryl Gates. Born in Glendale, in 1926, Gates was the son of an alcoholic plumber and his devout Mormon wife. Gates wanted to be a lawyer but didn't have the funds. He settled for a $290-a-month job with the police department.

Parker died in 1966. Gates worked his way through the ranks, placing first on every exam. In 1978, Gates became chief, and since then has become known nationwide for bringing the Parker principle of "proactive," military-style law enforcement into the modern era. He pioneered the SWAT team in America, and the use of the battering ram. One of his favored methods was the "pretext traffic stop," which called for motorists to be pulled over based on their "profile." Wholesale roundups of homeboys were employed in the ghettos, carried out by a special unit called CRASH.

Gates's rise coincided perfectly with the war on drugs; with law and order the Maypole around which politicians danced, his style of policing was an advertisement for government action, a tonic for suburban fears. He and other local generals operated with virtual carte blanche. "We must do whatever is necessary to deter those who would suppress us at home," he once told an audience of police boosters. "We are not just the first line of defense, ladies and gentlemen, we are the only line. But you can count on us. We will win this war."

Over the years, Gates has told many audiences many things. He told a Latino audience that Latino officers were not being promoted because they were lazy. Once, discussing the controversial "carotid choke hold," Gates suggested that blacks had died because "their veins or arteries do not open up as fast as they do on normal people." He told a U.S. Senate panel that "casual drug users should be shot." When his own son, a heroin addict, was jailed for robbing a pharmacy, Gates said, "He'll get no help from me."

Gates's attitude seemed to trickle down to the rank and file. A random review of MDT transmissions: "Sounds like monkey slapping time." "If you encounter these negros, shoot first, ask questions later." "Capture him, beat him, and treat him like dirt." "Shoot him twice for me."

***

CHP Officer Melanie Singer approached the white Hyundai with caution. Behind and all around, twenty-six other officers stepped gingerly out of patrol cars.

"What's your name?" Singer asked the driver.

"Glleeenn," he slurred, exhaling a pungent cloud of malt liquor.

Singer reeled, took a step back. "Get down on the ground, Glenn," she ordered, not unkindly.

Glenn, both hands out the window, looked quizzical, then hoisted himself out of the Hyundai. He seemed slow, a little stiff. He also seemed happy.

Glenn looked up at the helicopter, shielded his eyes from the blinding spotlight. He smiled and waved. He let out a full, deep belly laugh. Then he began to dance, shuffling his feet, a pitter-patter step. He smirked at Singer.

"Get down on the ground!" she commanded.

"Why you want me to get on the ground?" he asked. He danced a few more steps, then stopped.

He reached down with his right hand, fingers moving toward the back pocket of his pants.

"Get your hands away from you butt!" yelled Singer.

Glenn turned, about-face. He bent forward a little from the waist, grabbed a handful of his right buttock, jiggled.

Singer was flabbergasted. She drew her weapon. "Hit the ground!" she ordered.

"No. No!" came a deep voice. Singer cut her eyes right. A sergeant was stepping forward. Sergeant Stacey Koon, LAPD.

Koon was 40, a fifteen-year veteran of the department. Muscular, stern-faced, with a receding hairline, Koon was married to a nurse, the father of five children, a devout member of Our Lady of Perpetual Help Catholic Church. Neighbors remember the time a dog jumped his fence and entered his house. Koon had threatened the pet with his pistol.

Koon took an easy step forward, sized up the perp. He saw a big man, buffed out, very muscular. He appeared disoriented and unbalanced. Koon suspected PCP.

"Get back! We'll handle," rasped Koon to Singer. Then he addressed Glenn: "Get down on the ground!"

Koon pulled his Taser, a device that shoots darts connected by wires to a power source. Once the darts are implanted in skin, a 50,000-volt charge can be dispensed. "If you don't start following orders, I'm going to electrocute you!" he commanded.

Glenn dropped to all fours. To Koon, Glenn looked like a lineman set for the hike. Koon didn't know what this guy was going to do.

He might rush an officer, take his weapon, get him in a death grip—anything was possible.

"Now Koon noticed two other suspects in the car. He sensed a setup. He decided gunfire might be necessary. "Powell!" he barked like a platoon leader. "You're the designated shooter!" Then he ordered some other officers to get Pooh and Freddie G. out of the car.

Glenn, meanwhile, was on the ground. He appeared to be doing push-ups. Koon signaled. Cops swarmed. Powell went in with the handcuffs. As Powell tried to cuff him, Glenn rose up, throwing off officers like rag dolls, according to one cop, trying to get away, according to another. In either case, in the shuffle, Glenn bumped against Powell, almost knocking him off his feet. Powell, falling backward, thought this was it. He reached for his gun. . . .

Koon fired the Taser. He scored twice, back and side. Then he hit the hot switch: 50,000 volts.

Glenn screamed for a full five seconds. A witness would later say it sounded like a death wail. A cop would later say "wounded animal." Glenn began crawling, scuttling across the asphalt.

"Anyone else have a Taser?" Koon yelled. Others were yelling now too. "Get down!" "Lie down!" "Put your hands up!" "Put your hands behind you back, nigger!"

***

One hundred yards away, on the second floor of the Mountainback Apartments, George Holliday slid back the balcony door and stepped outside. No shoes, no shirt, it was cold. He tried to hold the camera still. The helicopter circled above, its 30 million-candlepower spotlight bathing everything in a grainy incandescent glow, as if the night had opened and the heavens were peeking through.

George peered through the viewfinder. Glenn was down on all fours, like the starting position in wrestling. Suddenly, he rolled to his right and got to his feet, a sit-out, a three-point escape. He ran one, two, three steps west toward the back bumper of the Hyundai.

"Powell and Wind," Koon barked. "Batons! Power strokes!"

Powell surged forward and cut off Glenn's angle. Earlier tonight, at baton training, Powell had been admonished for weakness. Now his PR-24 flashed down full stroke and connected with skull and face, crushing the bones around Glenn's eye like an eggshell. Glenn screamed, fell, blood began to flow.

Powell commenced pummeling at will, both hands on his baton, a grip like a baseball bat, a stroke like a golf club, back and forth, back and forth, swinging the two-foot black metal truncheon across Glenn's body. Head, neck, shoulders, back, kidneys, legs, ankles, feet. Ten, twelve, fifteen blows, in rapid succession.

Powell stopped. He stood poised over Glenn, breathing hard, weapon cocked just about his shoulder. For a moment, Glenn lay motionless. Then he groaned, turned his head. Powell wound up . . . a cop grabbed the top of his baton.

"Do you give? Do you give?" It was Koon. He came closer, manipulating the double wires from the Taser like a man trying to untangle the strings of a fallen kite. "Okay," barked Koon. "He gives." Melanie Singer sighed. It was over now. The perp had been subdued. Time to cuff him and get out of there.

Glenn pushed up off his stomach, rose to his knees and leaned back, like a prizefighter trying to get up from the canvas.

Powell commenced pummeling again. Wind started in too. Head, neck, shoulders, the whipsaw action, back and forth, back and forth. Powell was adrenalized. He saw the perp in a tunnel of light, so intent that he didn't even notice that his partner had joined in too. Wind was at Glenn's back, hitting kidneys and shoulder blades. He felt highly excited, transfixed, determined to hold up his side. He was frightened. He thought maybe he wasn't strong enough to hurt the guy. He stroked harder. Glenn's face split open. Blood splattered in a radius of five yards.

Meanwhile, Pooh and Freddie G. were on the other side of the car, on their stomachs in the grass, their heads turned away from the action. Pooh heard bones breaking, loud thumps, gushy sounds.

George Holliday was glued to the scene in his viewfinder. It was like a movie for real; you were riveted. He was just stuck there, thinking that this had to be filmed, just making sure that the camera was going. All he could think was, What did this guy do? What did he do to deserve this?

Beneath the balcony, twenty other residents of Mountainback stood watching. "Oh, my God! They're beating him to death!" cried one woman.

"They're stomping him like a bug!" shouted another.

"He's not even fighting back!"

"All them motherfuckers laughin'!"

In the road, Glenn moaned. "Please stop, please stop."

For ninety full seconds, Powell and Wind beat Glenn with their sticks. They beat a while. They stopped a while. A car drove by slowly, westbound. Glenn was scared for his life. It hurt real bad. Just keep breathing, Glenn, he told himself. The officers continued to pound. Powell was at his head, Wind at his feet, Koon in the center, controlling the wires. Glenn rolled back to front, trying to ward off the blows, lifting an arm here to cover his head, reaching down to cover his leg, rolling back to front, rolling away, rolling the whole length of the Hyundai, bumper to bumper, trying to get away, crying out in animal anguish, the cops still beating, beating, now on the head, now on the legs, now on the kidneys, whipsawing, kicking with heavy shoes.

Finally, it was over. Some of the cops swarmed. They pulled Glenn's arms behind his back, cuffed his wrists, hog-tied him, binding his hands to his feet with a nylon rope. Then, a couple of cops hauled him off to the side of the road, pulling him by his ankles, sliding him across the gravel on his chest, head dragging. Other cops stood silent, heads bent.

Through his viewfinder, full zoom, George could see the body language of guilt.

***

Within minutes, Koon was back in his patrol car, headed for the station house, and Larry Powell and Tim Wind were back in theirs, headed for the hospital. Once Glenn had been cuffed, most of the cops sped away. The rest left right after the ambulance crew hefted Glenn onto a stretcher, still hog-tied. As a joke, one of the officers at the scene pulled the sheet over Glenn's head. Glenn wondered, If this is what it is being dead, why do I feel this way?

As the Hyundai was being towed away, Pooh and Freddie G. were told they could go. They asked the cops where they were. The cops laughed. Crip country, they said. Then they drove away. "Shit!" said Freddie G., leaning on his crutch, watching the taillights recede. "They took my ID."

Pooh and Freddie G. walked over to the iron gate at Mountainback. George had stopped filming and gone inside, but several other residents remained. Pooh stuck his face through the fence and asked if they could use a telephone. They were directed to a pay phone at a gas station a few blocks away.

Now, in his car, Koon pulled the MDT in his direction, typed out a message to his watch commander. "You just had a big time use of force. Tased and beat the suspect of CHP pursuit, Big Time."

"Oh well. I'm sure the lizard didn't deserve it. HAHA. I'll let them know OK," typed the watch commander.

"I'm gonna drop by the station for a fresh Taser and darts," typed the sergeant. "Please have one ready at the desk."

***

T.J. and Melanie Singer walked into County Medical, looking for Glenn.

They found him on a gurney. Wind and Powell were nearby. Both appeared to be snoozing.

"You must be LAPD's designated hitter," T.J. Singer said to Larry Powell.

"I tired myself out hitting that guy," said Powell, nodding in Glenn's direction.

Now Glenn stirred, raised his head a few inches. Though Koon's report would list Glenn's injuries as "several facial cuts due to contact with asphalt, of a minor nature, a split inner lip," Glenn had been hit at least fifty-six times. His facial cuts required twenty-five stitches. One doctor would remark that it looked as if Glenn had been run over by a train. The bones in his cheek and around his eye were shattered.

Glenn's leg was broken, there was a huge bruise on his chest, he had wounds on his arms from trying to defend himself. Initial indications suggested some brain damage and possible loss of feeling in his mouth and on the side of his face. He'd been out cold now for a while. Earlier, in the emergency room, he'd leaned over to Koon and said, "I love you." Then he'd smiled and clapped.

Glenn stirred, regaining consciousness. "What happened?" he asked.

Powell walked over to Glenn. "We played a little baseball tonight, didn't we?" he said.

"What do you mean?"

"We played a little hardball, and you lost."

There was a silence awhile, then T.J. Singer spoke. "Why didn't you stop your car?" he asked Glenn.

"I was trying to get home to my wife, man."

***

And that was it, at least for the next thirty-six hours or so. The cops noted a minor fracas on their nightly report and went home to get some shut-eye. Glenn dozed in the lockup wing of the county hospital, stitched and plastered, heavily sedated. Glenn's brother Paul called the Foothill Division and said he wanted to file a complaint. The sergeant on duty refused to initiate an investigation. George Holliday took his videocam to the L.A. Marathon, then to a wedding.

On Monday, when the evening news came on, George got to thinking. Maybe somebody might want to see his video. He called Channel 5. They told him to bring it in.

By midnight on Tuesday, March 5, George's answering-machine tape had filled up with messages from the press. And by the next morning, when CNN aired the video and a crowd of reporters and cameras gathered outside George's balcony, the brutal beating of a motorist by LAPD cops had been broadcast from Austria to Zaire. Over and over and over the tape was played, the most sensational news footage to hit the airwaves since the war in the Persian Gulf. The image of Glenn cowering beneath Powell's and Wind's blows was burned onto America's retina, more powerful than any movie, real-life action drama, brutality so ugly that watching it made you wince.

The outrage was profound. George Bush made a comment. Jesse Jackson made a speech. Al Sharpton led a march. The FBI investigated, knocking on policeman's doors. The U.S. Department of Justice began a nationwide probe. Citizens called for the ouster of Los Angeles Mayor Tom Bradley, a black former cop. Bradley and others called for the resignation of Chief Gates. Gates joined the call for the ouster of Bradley.

Commissions were formed. Panels were seated, investigations and tribunals were convened. Gates was suspended. Gates went to court. Gates was restored. Gates called on the city to pay his legal bills. The city council sided with Gates. The Police Commission sided with Bradley, then sued the city council for money to discharge the powers granted them by the city charter. They went to court. Finally, Gates said he would retire in April 1992.

Experts opined about the psychology of group violence, the wantonness of the American spirit, the relative merits of "proactive" policing, the state of minority relations in the country.

In the meantime, indictments were handed down. Koon, Powell, Wind, and another officer, Ted Briseno, seen in the video stomping Glenn once with his boot, were all charged with assault with a deadly weapon and unnecessarily beating a suspect under the color of authority. Koon and Powell were also indicted for filing a false police report, and Koon was additionally charged with acting as an accessory to a cover-up. If convicted, Koon and Powell could be sentenced to a maximum of seven years, eight months in state prison. Wind faces a maximum of seven-year prison term. Briseno faces a max of four. Koon, Powell and Briseno were suspended from the force. Wind, a probationer, was fired, as were two L.A. Unified School District cops who happened upon the scene but did not file a report. T.J. and Melanie Singer both received written reprimands, for filing inadequate reports.

George Holliday experienced his fifteen minutes of fame. He appeared on *Geraldo*, in *People*, on a Japanese news show. Strangers wrote to offer free meals. Hollywood showed interest in buying the story of his life. Recently, a team of attorneys has drawn up a federal-copyright-infringement suit on George's behalf. The target of the suit has not yet been identified; a figure of $7 million has been mentioned.

Freddie G. was killed in a traffic accident involving alcohol. Pooh has been visited by bad dreams, is under psychiatric care, is suing the county. Shortly after the incident, Pooh was picked up for driving under the influence. His case is pending.

Glenn has become known as Rodney to the whole world. He has become something of a folk hero, maybe an antihero. Amid reports of depression, confusion, plastic surgery, counseling, pain, alienation of affection, and a long road to recovery, Glenn was stopped once by police for driving with an expired registration and no driver's license. He encountered the LAPD yet again, in an alley near the Sunset Strip, where he was receiving favors from a transvestite hooker in the front seat of his new Chevy Blazer. When under-cover cops approached his truck, Glenn sped off, almost hitting one of them. The police insisted that they had been tailing the hooker. Glenn's attorney insisted that police were attempting to gather discrediting evidence for the $83 million lawsuit Glenn has filed against the county.

Except for a brief press conference, following the release from the hospital, Glenn has declined to speak in public. What he was thinking that night, why he didn't just stop when T.J. and Melanie Singer first gave chase, remains a mystery, even to Glenn himself, say friends.

In the end, perhaps, it doesn't matter what Glenn was thinking, or even what Koon, Powell, Wind and the rest of the police officers were thinking. On a March night, on a lonely road in Los Angeles County, in the year 1991, certain ugly human truths were uncovered. Three minutes of 8-mm. videotape confirmed what many in America definitely knew, what many more in America probably knew but wanted to disbelieve.

Of all the millions of words that have been printed about the Rodney King Incident, as it has come to be known, several hundred came to the *Los Angeles Times* from a holy man named Thich Nhat Hahn. This is some of what he said:

People everywhere on the planet have seen the image of the policemen beating the young driver. The moment I first saw it, I saw myself as the one who was beaten, and I suffered. We were all beaten at the same time, we were all the victims of violence, anger, lack of understanding, lack of respect for our human dignity.

But looking more deeply, I was able to see that the policemen were also myself. Our society is full of hatred and violence. Everything is like a bomb ready to explode, and we are part of that bomb. If we are not mindful, then one day our child will be the one who is beaten, or the one doing the beating. It is our affair. We are not observers. We are participants.

THE REAL RICK ROSS IS NOT A RAPPER

Freeway Rick Ross didn't invent crack. But he probably did more than anyone else to cause its spread. The way he sees it, Ross was a banker in a shadow economy—an American capitalist in the grand tradition of our country's rags-to-riches folklore, bringing jobs and riches to his people and himself.

The *real Rick Ross is not a rapper.* That's what it says on his T-shirt, silk-screened attractively in two colors. The bold letters in black ink frame his image—bald, bearded, and somewhat bug-eyed with the fervor of his comeback. The gold ink requires a second stencil. Depicted on his head is a crown, cocked just so and perfectly aligned, the kingpin in exile, and below that his autograph, the excessively flamboyant signature of a man who once made millions a day selling cocaine but only began learning to read, behind bars, at age twenty-eight. Eventually, he would read himself to freedom.

On a sunny morning in southern California, Rick Ross is driving from his cramped but rent-free apartment along tony Ocean Avenue in Long Beach toward some pressing new business in blue-collar Riverside, an hour away. We're talking here about the real Rick Ross, born Ricky Donnell Ross in 1960, one of three Ricks from 'round the way, this one the Rick who stayed on Eighty-seventh Place where it dead-ended at the 110 Freeway, in the shadow of a massive concrete abutment where you could feel the earth vibrating beneath your feet, hence his nickname: Freeway Rick Ross ... as opposed to the rapper known as Rick Ross, a blubbery former college football player and corrections officer whose birth name is William Leonard Roberts II. When Roberts entered the music game, he appropriated the name and tattooed it across his fists: RICK RO$$. He rose to prominence rapping about a fictitious criminal past while the real Rick Ross, Freeway Rick Ross, a man iconic enough to have his name jacked, was serving a life sentence without the possibility of parole in a federal penitentiary.

Having brought suit against the rapper for copyright infringement and failed in several courts, Ross came up with the idea of these T-shirts. Over the past five months, with the help of a gangbanger turned silk-screener, he's printed five thousand. Offered in a rainbow of colors, in sizes up to 6XL, they are folded painstakingly and fitted into plastic bags by his older brother in a mini warehouse to which Ross has managed to secure the key, one in a seemingly endless series of fuzzy handshake arrangements through which he operates his portfolio of legal enterprises.

Everywhere he goes—to give testimony in a storefront church in Ontario; to lecture a law-school class at the University of Southern California; to make a personal appearance at an open-mic night in Inglewood; to have lunch at Denny's in Carson (he's a vegan; the chain features a garden burger); to attend a party for a Korean rapper who worships Ross as an American folk hero; to take a meeting at Warner Bros. studios in Burbank or with an Epic/Sony vice-president in Beverly Hills—Ross rolls behind him unselfconsciously a battered suitcase full of merch, the zipper toggles missing, his Willy Loman smile unwavering as he digs through the slippery packages to find the proper size and color, no charge for a photo. If you don't have the twenty dollars, more than likely he'll sell it for less. Taken by the moment, by the recognition and adulation, he'll often make it a gift.

If you meet Rick Ross and you tell him you're broke, broker even than he is at the moment—there is $11.15 left in his savings account—he'll spot you a ten-pack of T-shirts, a $200 value on the streets. (If you live out of town, he'll mail you a ten-pack; someone else donates postage from his company's postal machine.) His manufacturer's price is about four dollars per piece. Wholesale is ten dollars. On the Web the price is twenty-five dollars. Sell those shirts, pay him back a hundred dollars, and you get to keep the profit. If you're smart like Rick Ross, the real Rick Ross, Freeway Rick, you'll reinvest. Just like that, you're in business.

Back in the day, Ross would offer the same deal with crack cocaine—to start you out, he'd give you $100 worth for free, and you could sell it for $300. Between 1982 and 1989, federal prosecutors estimated, Ross bought and resold three tons of cocaine. In 1980 dollars, his gross earnings were said to be in excess of $900 million—with a profit of nearly $300 million. Converted roughly to present-day dollars: $2.5 billion and $850 million, respectively. As his distribution empire grew to include forty-two cities, the price he paid per kilo of powder cocaine dropped from as much as $60,000 to as low as $10,000. This was partially due to his exponentially increasing network of distributors, as Crips and Bloods struck out across the country to franchise the trade, spreading their gang culture with it ... and partially due to his sweetheart connection with a Nicaraguan national who would later be said to have ties to both the CIA and the contra rebels supported during the 1980s by the Reagan administration. (Later this same connect—Oscar Danilo Blandón—would be hired by the DEA as an informant; it was he who would bring Ross into the deal that led to his life sentence.)

Fueled by the findings of an investigation by San Jose Mercury News reporter Gary Webb in 1996, many would come to believe that the CIA had actually created the crack epidemic in America by allowing (or turning a blind eye to) massive shipments of cocaine into the country, the profits from which went to arming rebels fighting a Latin American regime disfavored by our government. Webb also theorized that much of the contra coke (cultivated in Colombia) ended up in the hands of Freeway Rick Ross.

Webb's revelations were aggressively attacked by the country's major newspapers, in reports heavy with unnamed government sources. Webb left the paper in disgrace; he was later found dead with two bullets in his head, an apparent suicide. An earlier inquiry led by then-senator John Kerry supported the substance of Webb's allegations, as did a 1998 report by the CIA's inspector general. Even many of those who vilified Webb now acknowledge that much of what he reported was true. A minority of the citizenry still believes there was genocidal intent in the CIA's actions—that the coke was deliberately funneled toward black ghettos as a way of decimating a troublesome population.

Deliberate or not, crack spread like a brush fire through the desiccated urban landscape, causing what USC law professor Jody Armour calls "the crack plague and its festering aftermath." Today, the ripples are still felt on all sociological levels; 30 percent of African-American males under thirty are currently incarcerated or on probation or parole. Along the way, crack also helped to enrich law-enforcement agencies and private security contractors and to elect politicians; being "tough on crime" became a necessary platform plank, a mind-set that would later dovetail into post-9/11 issues of domestic security. In 1986, when homicide rates due to gang warfare across the country had reached all-time highs, mandatory federal sentencing minimums were established, making the penalties for possession of crack by weight a hundred times more punitive than those for possession of powder cocaine. Many say this is one of the reasons for the disparities of race in our prison population. Only recently did President Barack Obama sign legislation reducing the crack-to-powder-coke ratio to 18 to 1. To date, various estimates place the cost of the four-decade-plus war on drugs between $500 billion and $4 trillion.

The way Rick Ross sees it, he was a banker in a shadow economy, working with the only currency available to a disenfranchised segment of society. By giving out unsecured microloans, he created jobs. By middling large quantities of this once-refined plant (similar to sugar or coffee, only illegal), he made himself and others wealthy—an American capitalist in the grand tradition of our country's rags-to-riches folklore. Working with gang leaders he'd known since grade school, both Crips and Bloods, Ross created a sales model—a foolproof recipe for cooking powder coke into crack using household materials; a chain of organization; an army of Dope Boys; and standardized curbside service techniques that were exported around the country and continued to evolve one step ahead of police and their increasingly well-stocked arsenal.

The real Rick Ross. Freeway Rick Ross. He didn't invent crack. But he probably did more than anyone else to cause its spread. Just Say No. The War on Drugs. Mandatory Minimums. The Wire. RICK RO$$. This is his legacy. Say hello to my little friend.

***

At the moment, Freeway Rick Ross is sitting behind the wheel of a salvaged Hyundai Santa Fe with 169 grand on the odometer. He is traveling seventy miles per hour in the middle lane of the 110 Freeway, heading for the 91 Freeway, chatting nonstop to a series of callers on a BlackBerry cell phone with a cracked face that the mother of his two youngest children—Mychosia Nightingale, a former Army sergeant who did three tours in Iraq—found for him on Craigslist for twenty-nine dollars. (Ross doesn't do computers.)

The steering wheel vibrates beneath his driving hand. The wheels of the vehicle are slightly out of alignment; it was purchased at auction on his behalf by another of his partners, this one a reformed bank robber who is helping him learn the business of flipping low-end cars. So far this week, Ross has sold two cars, one of them the sedan his brother was driving; after repair expenses, he's cleared nearly two grand. There's a nice Honda waiting in Riverside; all it needs is a new air bag and it's ready for Craigslist. Prior to jumping on the freeway, Ross stopped at a junkyard and scored.

By any account, going legit hasn't been easy. After his release from prison in 2009 (more on that below), Ross tried long-distance trucking. He was up to owning seven rigs when the repair bills crippled him. Then, he says, two of his cousins ran off with the last two viable trucks. Next, he tried the hair business—human hair for extensions. Another cousin, who was supposed to go to India to buy more hair, ran off with a suitcase full of money.

Ever upbeat, Ross keeps trying. Among projects he's pursuing: a storefront for the T-shirts. A literacy campaign. A social-media campaign (freewaysocialmedia.com). A rap label. (If you want to be signed, you have to sell T-shirts.) A sports training and management agency specializing in troubled athletes. An energy pill. (His potential partner made a fortune selling faux marijuana and bath salts.) By far his biggest hopes lie in Hollywood. Ross has a partnership stake in a documentary about his life, Crack in the System, by the filmmaker Marc Levin. He's also shopping his biopic. It was written by Nick Cassavetes, a cowriter of Blow; Nick Cannon has signed on to play Freeway Rick Ross. So far, Ross hasn't found anyone willing to give him $36 million to make the film.

Likewise, the T-shirts. He sold $1,500 worth his first month and reinvested everything. The problem he's got right now is re-ups—he is owed something like $4,000. Apparently, his corps of street salespeople have discovered a slight problem with Ross's model—T-shirts don't sell like crack.

Ross's cell phone is set to speaker, propped on his right shoulder to avoid another ticket. There's a spare battery charging in a broken phone in the cupholder; a third battery floats loose in the pocket of his jeans, the same pair the government issued him on the day he walked out of the federal prison in Texarkana, in northeast Texas, after serving fourteen years of a reduced sentence. The calls come in every few minutes: acolytes and sycophants, old homies and new connects, possible business partners, members of the media.

"What up what up what up?" Ross answers, ever upbeat. "Talk to me. Who dat?"

This particular caller has been highly anticipated. He's from a television show—Russell Brand's late-night talk fest, Brand X. The hugely popular English comedian is taping his last installment of the season tonight. Ross is scheduled to appear.

As Rick has been learning, it's one thing to be mobbed by a crowd of adoring brothers and sisters at the giant City of Hope church, or at Earlez Grille on Crenshaw Boulevard, or at the corner of Eighty-first and Hoover, a former weed and PCP spot where Ross became the first street dealer to offer ready rock for sale to the public. (His initial customers were dealers, known as D Boys, the D for dope. They liked to mix a little crack into their marijuana blunts—street name: coco-puffs.)

But it's quite another to gain acceptance from the mainstream—especially when you're trying to raise $36 million for a film. This shot on national TV is just what he needs, a big-time arena in which to push his shirts and his various campaigns, a chance to explain a little bit about himself, to put things in context, to explain his situation—how he was really more of an entrepreneur giving out microloans than a drug pusher peddling death. How the CIA practically put the drugs in his hands.

He puts the caller on speaker. He sounds superfriendly; the two have spoken before. The routine of arrival at the studio is explained.

The names of Ross's greenroom entourage are locked down on the list. A medium-sized Real Rick Ross T-shirt is requested. Then talk turns to plans for the segment.

"We'd like to have you show the audience how to make crack," the caller says.

Ross's large and expressive eyes seem to bulge out of their sockets. "You want me ... to come on your show and cook crack?" He looks as if he's about to cry.

"Yes!" enthuses the caller. His tone is reminiscent of a cheerleader pumping a fist in the air. "Can you tell me what we'll need?"

***

The 110 Freeway links the port of Long Beach with downtown L.A. It runs through the eastern side of the city, paralleling the coastline, passing near the Watts Towers, the L.A. Memorial Coliseum, the USC campus, and the Staples Center before merging with Interstate 10, a gateway to the rest of the nation.

The harbor is one of the world's busiest. Massive ships arrive daily, decks stacked impossibly high with colorful containers, which are unloaded by giant erector-set roustabouts and set like toys onto rail cars and tractor rigs. Leaving Long Beach, the 110, also known as the Harbor Freeway, runs through blighted communities that once housed hundreds of thousands of blue-collar workers, many of them African-Americans who'd immigrated from the South in successive waves after World War II, seeking jobs and a better life. Today the area is best known for gangs, drugs, and economic despair. After the 1992 riots, people of color began to refer to a place called Soweto South of Pico Boulevard—the geographical line of demarcation between the haves and have-nots in Los Angeles.

A number of years ago, the 110 Freeway was widened. By eminent domain, construction claimed the house, at 430 West Eighty-seventh Place, where Ross grew up. Today if you go there, the ground still trembles. Homeless people live in makeshift tents beneath the overpass.

One evening in 1979, when Ross was nineteen and the modest clapboard house still stood, Ross arrived home with his buddy Ollie

"Big Loc" Newell to find the usual friends and family hanging out in the garage that Ross and his brother had converted into a bedroom/clubhouse. There was a sofa and chairs, a TV, a rug on the concrete floor.

The house was shared by Ross's aunt and his mother, Annie Mae Mauldin, the daughter of an east-Texas sharecropper, a no-nonsense woman who'd lost her left eye to a broomstick in a fight with a man. Ross's father, Sonny Ross, a former Army cook and later a pig farmer, came from similar roots. Rick would have no relationship with him until after Rick's first stint in prison. He ended up bunking for a time with the old man, the only qualified (and available) non-felon in Texas who was able to offer him shelter under the terms of his release. Having missed out on significant portions of the lives of his own five older children—by far the most painful part of his incarceration, he says—Rick made amends with Sonny before he died. Of particular interest to Ross was the time his dad spent, during his younger days, as a moonshiner. Unlike his son, Sonny tended to quit stuff when it got too hot. (He tried to live in L.A. for a time but returned after he was held up at gunpoint by two women while working the overnight shift in a gas station in South Central.)

Ross and his mother came to South Central in 1963, when he was three. Left behind in Texas, along with the yellow shack in which he'd grown up, were his brother David, his bicycle, and his dog, Pooch, the things he loved most in the world, according to his autobiography, which he wrote in prison with the help of his cellmate, who helped teach him to read using makeshift flashcards. At first, Ross and his mother lived with her brother, George, and his wife. One night George became enraged and attacked his wife and sister. As little Ricky looked on in terror, his mom pulled a handgun from her purse and killed Uncle George. After what Ross remembers as a long and painful separation, Mauldin was released from jail and mother and son were reunited.

Throwing in with George's wife, Mauldin bought the house on Eighty-seventh Place. Mauldin cleaned office buildings, did landscaping, worked for a lawyer soliciting auto-accident cases. Eventually, the family went on welfare. Ross remembers collecting canned food from looted stores after the Watts riots. Mauldin is now in her mid-eighties, a sprightly woman with a quick laugh who drives a minivan and likes to gamble in a nearby casino. She remembers Ricky being embarrassed by government handouts, always hustling. He cut lawns, sold lemonade, pumped gas for tips, shoplifted, ran errands for neighborhood pimps. At Manchester Elementary, Ross wasn't so industrious. He fought with classmates, sassed teachers—the little guy with the big temper. Even though he couldn't read, he was promoted every year.

"There weren't no bankers or lawyers in my neighborhood to learn from," Ross says. "The pimps and the hustlers was my role models. There was experts on burglary, there was experts on how to rob somebody at the ATM, how to get a gun, how to file off the serial numbers—all this information was readily available in our community. Criminal enterprise was the only work we had."

As a boy, Ross spent many of his summers back in Texas, on modest farms owned by Mauldlin uncles. (For much of his life, Ross hated his name. He wished to be a Mauldlin like his cousins.) "If you wanted extra food for dinner, my uncle would tell you okay, but you'd have to put in extra work the next day to pay for it." Later, as a drug dealer, he'd demonstrate the same ethic. "If you called me at twelve o'clock at night, I'd go," he once said. "Another guy, he might be with his girlfriend, 'Oh, I can't come tonight.' Another guy, he be sitting there smoking a cigarette. He can't do nothing until he finish smoking that cigarette. But Rick don't smoke cigarettes. Rick can move right now. He don't have a beer can in his hands or a bottle of liquor. That's the only difference between me and most of my friends in the drug business—my discipline."

Ross attended middle school during the early seventies, around the same time the Crips street gang was being founded by a 17-year-old weightlifter named Stanley "Tookie" Williams III. Started initially as a sort of neighborhood-watch brigade by muscle heads who prided themselves on a fly style of dress, the Crips would mutate across South Central (and further spawn the rival Bloods). One day at Bret Harte Junior High, after putting his books into his locker, Ross turned around to find himself staring down the barrel of a .38-caliber pistol—Ross could see clearly the bullet inside the chamber. Somehow his homies defused the incident, but Ross was deeply shaken. He resolved to never join a gang. "I figured there had to be something better for me out there. I just didn't know what it was yet."

As it happened, his answer came in the unlikely form of a tennis racket, when a man showed up to hold a clinic at nearby Manchester Park. Ross went to the park nearly every day, despite the fact that he and his pals had once discovered a mutilated body floating in the swimming pool. (The memory would haunt him for years, as would his uncle's shooting, crippling him at times with debilitating symptoms of post-traumatic shock. In later years Ross would never be known for violence. If someone beat him on a deal, he didn't order a hit. Instead, he'd find inspiration, redouble his efforts to succeed. He'd think, *That motherfucker gonna be sorry when I blow the fuck up.*)

At first, given racquets and balls, Ross and his friends ran roughshod across the courts, improvising primitive games of baseball and street hockey. Eventually the instructor prevailed, and the ruffians were tamed. Everybody could see it instantly: Freeway Rick had talent.

Too small for football or basketball, the quick and tenacious Ross found in tennis a legit place to excel. By ninth grade he was recruited to play for Dorsey High School, a magnet school in Baldwin Hills, an exclusive residential area south of downtown known as the black Beverly Hills.

Ross climbed the depth chart and eventually garnered all-city honors at Dorsey; he even went so far as to attempt the SATs—a bravado effort that ended dismally. Eventually, he dropped out before receiving his diploma. As his jock friends went off to college scholarships, Ross ended up playing for the tennis team at Los Angeles Trade-Technical College, where he was studying auto upholstery, inspired by his newfound passion for lowriders. He bought a 1966 Impala convertible and set about restoring and customizing it—juiced, lifted, and sporting fancy rims, the vehicle could hop three feet off the ground. He joined a car club and attended regular carhops at Church's Chicken on Vermont Avenue and Century Boulevard. From there, caravans would form, sometimes a mile long—music blaring, cars bouncing, rims gleaming, the rear-ends of some vehicles dragging purposely to create a rooster tail of sparks, called flashing. To pay for his hobby, Ross fell into a network of auto thieves who became known as the Freeway Boys. He also became part owner of a chop shop.

Around the spring of 1982, Ross was arrested for the first time and charged with possession of stolen auto parts. Free on bail and awaiting trial, he got a call, as Ross tells it, from his old friend Mike, a running back who'd left town for a football scholarship to San Jose State University.

Mike was staying in the guesthouse of a nice place in Sugar Hill, an area popular with wealthy black folks prior to Baldwin Hills. It had its own kitchen and everything. Ross had never even had his own room.

Greeting Ross and his boy Ollie at the door, Mike pulled out a plastic baggie filled with white paper bindles. He removed one and opened it—inside was a small amount of white powder that sparkled beneath the lamplight. At the time, the most common drugs to use or sell in the ghetto were black-tar heroin, marijuana, and PCP—phencyclidine, a powerful anesthetic. The only time Ross had even heard of cocaine was in the movie Superfly.

"This is worth fifty dollars," Mike said.

"Stop lying," Ross laughed.

"Man, no joke. They going crazy over this stuff. All of the entertainers are doing it. All the white people are doing it."

"Well, if it worth that much, I'm gonna find a way to get rich," Ross proclaimed.

"Take this and see what you can do with it," Mike said. He handed over the half-gram bindle.

Now Ross and Ollie arrived home to find the usual suspects collected in the garage bedroom/clubhouse. There was Ross's cousin Kenny, his friends Group and Cruz Dog, a couple of others. In Ross's mind, "these guys was supposed to be the ones in our little circle who knew what was going on in the streets. The players, the down hustlers, the street-smart guys—these was them."

Ollie bolted the interior door, and Ross produced with some ceremony the little packet of cocaine. He opened it on the table.

The scent was vaguely medicinal, like something you might smell in the emergency room. Everybody stood dumbfounded, just looking at one another.

Cruz Dog was one of Ross's oldest homies, a fleet wide receiver turned fearless Crip soldier Ross had known since Manchester Elementary.

He pushed back his cap and scratched his head, spoke for the group. "What is it, cuz?"

***

Ross and Ollie drove around the hood, seeing what they could find out about this new drug, seeking wisdom from elders. They asked an OG named Bonnie and another named Big Al, but they didn't know nothing. Eventually, they ran into Martin the pimp. Martin knew all about freebasing. He demonstrated how to cook the powder into crack using baking soda—he produced a small nugget that looked like a white aquarium stone.

Then Martin demonstrated how to smoke it. (It made a loud crackling sound when lit; some say that's the origin of the name.)

An hour later, Ross and Ollie were back at the house on Eighty-seventh Place, stewing on the front porch. The drugs were gone. They owed Mike fifty dollars. Ollie wanted payback.

"Man, you can't kill Martin," Ross said. "That's the OG man, everybody in the hood gonna be mad."

Then, all of a sudden, Martin pulled up in front of the house. He was riding with Big Mouse, one of the original Crips. The two approached the porch. Martin's eyes looked wide and a little crazy. Ross steeled himself.

The old pimp greeted Ross like a long-lost friend. He took Ross's hand in a soul shake: "Man, I got you a customer," he enthused.

When Mike had first pulled out the coke in the guesthouse, Ross snorted a couple of lines and was unimpressed. In powder form the effects were subtle. But after watching Martin cook the crack and compulsively smoke it—and return an hour later in an urgent search for more, with financing in tow—Ross knew he'd discovered an opportunity. Ross wasn't the first to cook and deal crack—a mass-produced form of what others were calling freebase. Crack was documented by UCLA researchers as early as 1974 in the San Francisco area. At the same time, Ross was experimenting with sales of ready rock, so were dealers and users in New York and Miami. Along with a source of heat and some water, "a saucer, a glass, a paper towel, and Arm & Hammer baking soda are about all that is needed" to cook crack, according to a physician who testified in 1979 before a U. S. House Select Committee.

In the beginning crack was called freebase. Early crack was the exact same product, only mass produced. (Later Ross would learn, from a leader of the Grape Street Crips, of a substance called "Blow Up" that could be added to the recipe to increase the weight of each batch. With that modification to the process, earnings became exponentially higher—and the quality of the buzz exponentially lower.) An interesting note: At one time, crack had no name. It was considered an unusable by-product. In order to test the purity of a shipment, dealers would cook a batch of crack, a simple chemical procedure, like a high school chemistry experiment demonstrating precipitation. If you cooked a gram of coke with a certain amount of baking soda, and then yielded a half gram of crack (the precipitate was called "come back"), you knew your load was fifty percent pure. Somewhere along the line, someone took stuff out of the trash and tried smoking it. One can only imagine their surprise.

Ross could see immediately that crack had considerable marketing advantages over coke. A five-dollar hit created an orgasmic high, somewhat akin to the erotic full body rush of heroin. It also created a powerful urge to chase the first rush every fifteen minutes or so with another hit (interestingly, the Blow Up did not seem to decrease at all the temporal addictive effects). In crack form, coke was no longer water soluble or subject to melting—before the cops got wise, the D Boys would carry their loose rocks under their tongues to avoid discovery in searches. By 1980, when the comedian Richard Pryor set himself on fire cooking freebase (he preferred a posher method using ether), the world became aware of this new and dangerous drug. The death of collegiate basketball star Len Bias of a cocaine overdose further moved the drug into prominence. (Crack use was never proven in his case; more likely the Celtics #1 draft choice had been snorting powder.)

At first, Ross middled the coke for Mike, without commission, just to learn the ropes. Then he discovered that his upholstery teacher, who lived in Baldwin Hills, was also into coke. He had connections to Nicaraguan dealers. Ross started buying and selling more and more product. He paid Martin the pimp to cook each batch into crack; in time Ross figured out the simple process himself.

Thereafter, whenever Ross recruited a new subdealer, he'd teach him how to cook. He wasn't afraid to go into a hostile neighborhood to seek out a leader and make a deal. "I wasn't a Crip or a Blood. I was the man with the dope and the opportunity," Ross says.

He'd front as much as a kilo to a new distributor—anything to open a new market. He seemed to have a primitive and almost apriori knowledge of marketing and economics. In his prison-written book he writes of the epiphany of realizing that buying something in bulk was always cheaper than buying only one, a notion unknown to a kid who grew up surviving between welfare checks. Later, Ross would always make sure to stock up on inventory before the first and fifteenth of the month, when the government checks were distributed. He also had the discipline to reinvest his profits. At one point early in the game, Ollie and another guy, who was working with them in partnership, took large chunks of their profit shares and bought brand new vehicles, one a Cadillac, the other a tricked-out Ford van. "Instead of buying fancy stuff, I took my money, and I went and bought more and more dope—and eventually the dealer told them they was too small time and had to buy their dope from me. So, then I was getting a lower price, plus I was making money on all they shit, too," Ross explains.

Eventually Ross was introduced to a Nicaraguan named Oscar Danilo Blandón. A former marketing director in Nicaragua, Blandón and his wife were forced to flee their country in 1979 when the Cuban-aided Sandinista rebels defeated the U.S.-trained army of Nicaraguan dictator Anastasio Somoza and took over the country.

Dealing with Blandón, Ross seemed to have virtually unlimited access to drugs. By age twenty-three, Ross says, he was a millionaire; throughout the mid-eighties, he moved hundreds of pounds of cocaine powder a day. "I couldn't sell the shit fast enough. I wanted more, more, more. It's like I was worried it was going to run out," Ross says.

Ross was the prototype of a crack kingpin. He wore a bullet-proof vest and carried a 9mm, fathered five babies with four different women, kept himself surrounded by a posse of workers connected by state of the art walkie-talkies, ordered up bootleg designer furnishings for his motel (which he gave to his mom to run), bought an apartment building, sponsored a semipro basketball team, bought new pews for his mom's church, had so much cash he had to hire people to count it—there's a story about his mom finding his stash in his bedroom closet; it took an entire day to count, $2.8 million. After he bought new rims for the basketball courts at Manchester Park, the Los Angeles Department of Recreation and Parks gave him a plaque, expressing "deepest appreciation for your generous donation."

But he was never flashy. Only his intimates knew who he was, what he looked like. He kept his head down, wore T-shirts and jeans, was driven around in a beater of an automobile. He kept no particular residence. He didn't even have his own clothes closet. He stayed different nights at his motel or at the cribs of his different baby mommas. He'd wake up in the morning and put on whatever new clothes his women had bought for him while they were out spending his money on themselves and his kids. (Ross spent a lot of time with his kids when they were young, running and working out, teaching them all to play tennis; several of his sons would end up joining the gang life and running afoul of the law; his eldest daughter works at a CVS drug store.)

As he does today, Ross spent most of his time in a car, riding back and forth on the 110 Freeway and the other massive concrete roadbeds that crisscross the inland empire, checking on his different operations—if ever a childhood nickname grew up with the man, it was his. For a long time, the Freeway Rick Task Force—a squad of hardened drug cops from the L.A. County Sheriff's Department dedicated to his capture—actually had no idea what he looked like. On several occasions Ross walked away from police operations planned for the express purpose of capturing him—since an early age, he'd been known for his quickness, both on the tennis court and also down a dark alley and over a fence.

In 1988, a load of coke bound for his lucrative new territory in Cincinnati was detected by a drug-sniffing dog at a bus station in New Mexico. The drugs were traced to Ross; he was arrested. Federal indictments in Cincinnati, Los Angeles, and Tyler, Texas, were handed down. Ross pleaded guilty to cocaine-trafficking charges and received a mandatory ten-year prison sentence, which he began serving in 1990.

Around this time, a federal investigation into the sheriff's office was uncovering massive corruption. Dozens of narcotics officers were convicted of beating suspects, stealing drug money, and planting evidence. Ross testified for the government. In return he served only four years and nine months of his sentence.

Back home at thirty-four, Rick got a job hauling trash. His major efforts were devoted to an old theater in South Central he wanted to convert into a youth center/recording studio/performance space. While he'd been away in prison, holding on to the theater and his other remaining assets had been costing him nearly fifteen grand a month. With all the money spent on lawyers for himself and his workers, he was nearly broke. He'd paid the owner of the theater $900,000 up front and $6,000 a month while incarcerated. Now Ross was behind in the payments; the owner was threatening to foreclose. Everything else was gone. Ross was determined not to lose the theater, too.

Right about this time, Ross received a call from his old business partner, Blandón.

In late 1990 or 1991, Blandón was arrested by the LAPD with a suitcase full of cash—only to be bailed out by the U. S. Justice Department, which said he was part of a money-laundering case. Then, Blandón was arrested by the DEA for conspiracy to distribute cocaine.

While probation officers recommended a life sentence and a $4 million fine, the prosecution argued that Blandón was "extraordinarily valuable in major DEA investigations of Class I drug traffickers," and recommended forty-eight months and no fine. Less than a year later Blandón was freed. In a memo to a judge, the prosecutor wrote that Blandón had "almost unlimited potential to assist the United States ... as a full-time, paid informant after his release from prison."

Ross was a little surprised to hear from Blandón, but they'd always done beautiful business together. Ross and a friend drove to Blandón's downtown L.A. restaurant. After they chatted and caught up, Blandón got to his point. "The Colombians are on my back," he told Ross. He owed money; he had a shipment he needed to sell. "Why go around begging all these people for money for your theater when you can make it all at once?" Blandón asked.

Reluctantly or not, Ross found a buyer; as middleman, he was to receive a commission of $300,000 on a hundred-kilo sale. The deal went down in a shopping-center parking lot near San Diego on March 2, 1995. The DEA and local authorities swooped in. Ross's arrest netted Blandón more than $45,000 in government rewards and reimbursements. Ross was found guilty of conspiring to sell cocaine that had been provided by the DEA, in a deal set up by the DEA, a typical drug-war scenario. Ross received what was identified as his third felony strike, and with it a sentence of life in prison without possibility of parole.

Over the next few years Ross, who had learned to read only during his first stretch in jail, painstakingly read every business and self-help book in the prison library—during a fourteen-year period, he boasts, he devoured more than three hundred books. His trilogy of favorites: Think and Grow Rich, by Andrew Carnegie disciple Napoleon Hill; The Richest Man in Babylon, by George Samuel Clason; and As a Man Thinketh, by James Allen. Eventually, Ross held study groups with other inmates, spreading the word of economic self-sufficiency and can-do capitalism among the brothers. If we can be so successful selling crack, Ross preached, why can't we use the same skills toward legitimate business?

In late 1995, inmate 05550-045 was visited by journalist Gary Webb. Webb's Mercury News series, "Dark Alliance," was published in August 1996, and later became a book. Webb charged that the U. S. government had secretly allowed shipments of cocaine into the country in order to finance the purchase of weapons needed for the contra rebels to fight the leftist Sandinistas who'd taken over Nicaragua. Ross was portrayed as an unwitting pawn in a game of international covert politics.

After leaving his job in disgrace and watching his marriage dissolve, Webb methodically sold off his possessions and committed suicide in December 2004. According to the coroner's report, on his first attempt to shoot himself in the head, the father of three children missed the mark—instead he suffered a nonfatal wound. He placed the muzzle of his .38-caliber pistol against his head a second time and pulled the trigger.

Meanwhile, Ross sued, asking for more than $5 million in damages from the government. Although his case was rejected, his profile was raised mightily in a black community that had seized upon the notion that a government conspiracy was to blame for the plague of crack. In the people's mythology, the kingpin had become the victim, an anti-hero, and a martyr.

Stuck in prison with a life sentence, Ross "started consuming myself with reading law books," he says. "I started reading them the same way I'd sold drugs. When the library opened every morning, I was there standing in line. If I missed lunch, I missed lunch. I would take all of the money I could muster up and make copies of the law books, because they wouldn't let us take them back to our cells."

One day Ross found what he thought he was looking for. He'd received the life sentence for being convicted of a third federal crime—his third strike. But technically, he believed, he had only two strikes. Since his charges from the Texas and Ohio convictions had arisen from the commission of the same federal crime, how could they account for two separate strikes?

Excited, Ross called his lawyer, who shot him down. Ross got a court-appointed attorney. In 1998, the Ninth Circuit Court of Appeals agreed with Ross's jailhouse interpretation of the law. Ross's life sentence was reduced to twenty years. He ended up serving fourteen.

On May 4, 2009, he walked out of Texarkana prison into the arms of his woman, Sergeant Mychosia Nightingale. She'd seen Ross on a documentary about crack; she'd written, he'd urged her to read his favorite books. Facing a fourth deployment to Iraq, Nightingale quit the Army and drove from Georgia to Texarkana to pick him up. She spent the week sleeping in her SUV, waiting for him with a duffel bag of new clothes. Today they have two toddlers. He's already teaching them how to swing a tennis racket.

***

The real Rick Ross, Freeway Rick Ross, is southbound on the 110 toward home—this time he's riding behind the driver of a gleaming white Escalade limo provided by the producers of Brand X, wearing a custom REAL RICK polo shirt that his silk-screener had made up special for his appearance on national TV.

Though Ross had fretted the entire day over the producer's request that he cook crack on TV—eager to please, he'd reluctantly given the caller a list of ingredients, including a Bunsen burner and procaine, an anesthetic that in his experience would cook up very much like crack—Russell Brand never asked him to do so. Instead, Ross was trotted out before the studio audience like an old prizefighter and heralded as the "Donald Trump of crack." Though it's not what Ross was looking for—to be at once lionized and lampooned—it is probably a decent characterization. At the end of the segment, Brand could be heard blurting out something about cooking crack on national television; clearly, cooler heads had prevailed on this last episode before cancellation.

"All these interviews I do every day, all the meetings I take, all the hands I shake, all the pictures, hopefully it amounts to stuff," Ross says, slouching deeply in the seat of the Escalade limo, reflecting on the day's events. He sounds a little tired. It is nearly midnight, another long day.

"I just have to keep pressing and pressing and, you know, fight through all the little things. In the drug business I became an expert at drugs. I knew who sold drugs in Compton, in Watts, on the West Side, in the Jungle. And everybody knew me. But when it comes to Hollywood and this other stuff, I don't know it yet. It's like that Hollywood producer. After that long meeting and we was leaving, he laughed, and he said to everybody, 'Why am I shaking hands with this drug dealer?'"

Outside Ross's window, a police cruiser pulls even with the Escalade. The cop riding shotgun appears to be pointing at Ross, though this is impossible, given the fancy blacked-out windows in the limo. Ross has a recurring dream in which he's asleep in one of his old rock houses and a battering ram is knocking down the wall. He still wakes up sometimes not knowing where he is—twenty of his fifty-three years have been spent in cells in different facilities. He knows he's lucky he's not still behind bars.

Ross gestures toward the cops. "Don't you wanna know what they're thinking?"

"You don't have to worry about what they're thinking," I tell him.

"Not no more. Not like I used to," he says. In a month's time, he'll finally land a deal for a miniseries about his life—not the deal he wanted, but at least something he believes will pay off. He smiles big and his eyes bug gleefully, a little bit proud of himself.

"I ain't going to jail tonight."

PERMISSIONS

"The Rise and Fall of a Super Freak" was first published in a shorter, different form in *Rolling Stone*, June 27, 1996. In 2003 it was published in *Scary Monsters and Super Freaks*. Reprinted with permission from the author.

"Requiem for a Gangsta" was first published in a shorter, different form in *GQ*, November 1995. In 2003 it was published in *Scary Monsters and Super Freaks*. Reprinted with permission from the author.

"Damn! They Gonna Lynch Us!" was first published in a shorter, different form in *GQ*, October 1991. In 2003 it was published in *Scary Monsters and Super Freaks*. Reprinted with permission from the author.

"The Real Rick Ross is Not a Rapper" was first published in a shorter, different form in *Esquire*, September 2013. In 2015 it was published in *Stoned Again*. Reprinted with permission from the author.

ABOUT THE AUTHOR

Mike Sager is a best-selling author and award-winning reporter. A former *Washington Post* staff writer and contributing editor to *Rolling Stone*, he has written for *Esquire* for more than thirty years. Sager is the author or editor of more than a dozen books, including anthologies, novels, a biography, and textbooks. In 2010 he won the National Magazine Award for profile writing. A number of his stories have inspired films and documentaries; he is editor and publisher of The Sager Group LLC. For more information, please see www.MikeSager.com.

ABOUT THE PUBLISHERS

NeoText is a publisher of quality fiction and long-form journalism. Visit the NeoText website at NeoTextCorp.com.

The Sager Group was founded in 1984. In 2012 it was chartered as a multimedia content brand, with the intent of empowering those who create art—an umbrella beneath which makers can pursue, and profit from, their craft directly, without gatekeepers. TSG publishes books; ministers to artists and provides modest grants; and produces documentary, feature, and commercial films. By harnessing the means of production, The Sager Group helps artists help themselves. For more information, please see TheSagerGroup.net.

ALSO BY MIKE SAGER

NONFICTION

Scary Monsters and Super Freaks:
Stories of Sex, Drugs, Rock 'n' Roll, and Murder

Revenge of the Donut Boys: True Stories of Lust, Fame, Survival,
and Multiple Personality

The Someone You're Not:
True Stories of Sports, Celebrity, Politics & Pornography

Stoned Again:
The High Times and Strange Life of a Drugs Correspondent

Vetville: True Stories of the U.S. Marines at War and at Home

The Devil and John Holmes - 25th Anniversary Author's Edition:
And Other True Stories of Drugs, Porn and Murder

Janet's World:
The Inside Story of Washington Post Pulitzer Fabulist Janet Cooke

Travels with Bassem:
A Palestinian and a Jew Find Friendship in a War-Torn Land

The Lonely Hedonist:
True Stories of Sex, Drugs, Dinosaurs and Peter Dinklage

Tattoos & Tequila:
To Hell and Back with One of Rock's Most Notorious Frontmen

Shaman:
The Mysterious Life and Impeccable Death of Carlos Castaneda

Hunting Marlon Brando: A True Story

A Boy and His Dog in Hell: And Other True Stories

FICTION

Deviant Behavior, A Novel

High Tolerance, A Novel

Visit TheSagerGroup.net for more titles and authors

www.ingramcontent.com/pod-product-compliance
Lightning Source LLC
Chambersburg PA
CBHW022008120526
44592CB00034B/747